churches of Venice
the museum in the city

Chorus Marsilio

'No city in the world has a more glorious Bible than Venice', said John Ruskin, impassioned traveller and admirer of Venetian art. The Bible he was referring to was that comprising the extraordinary works of religious art in the churches of Venice, testimony to a thousand years of art, faith and history.
These works were the fruit of enlightened patronage and highly skilled hands which, in producing art of unrepeatable beauty, also very effectively opened up the holy scriptures to a people with little propensity for reading.
The churches of Venice and their art treasures are now the inestimable patrimony of mankind, and Chorus aims to make known the full splendour of history, beauty and spirituality that still survives between these ancient walls through its expansive project for their appreciation and protection. It intends welcoming visitors to these places and offering them a tour – illustrated in the pages of this guide which brings together fifteen jewels of architecture in an ideal compendium – in discovery of highly celebrated works and of secret, charming, often unknown parts of the city.

Don Aldo Marangoni
President
Chorus - Associazione Chiese di Venezia

PROMOV
Promovenezia S.c.a.r.l.
Castello 4421
30122 Venezia

with assistance from
Regione Veneto
L.R. n.13/13.03.94

Scientific coordination
Martina Mian
Luca Baldin

Translated by
David Graham

Note
Works marked by an asterisk (*)
will be displayed in the place indicated
on a date to be decided

Kind thanks to the authors of the Marsilio Guides
Venezia dal museo alla città
and Cameraphoto Arte, Venice
for its assistance

Photography
© Cameraphoto Arte, Venice
Fotolaboratorio dei Dogi, Venice

Graphic design
Tapiro, Venice

Layout
Daniela Albanese

Cover: Jacopo Robusti called Tintoretto
Presentation of the Virgin at the Temple, 1552-53,
detail Venice, church of Madonna dell'Orto

ISBN 88-317-88-317-8026-3

www.marsilioeditori.it

Contents

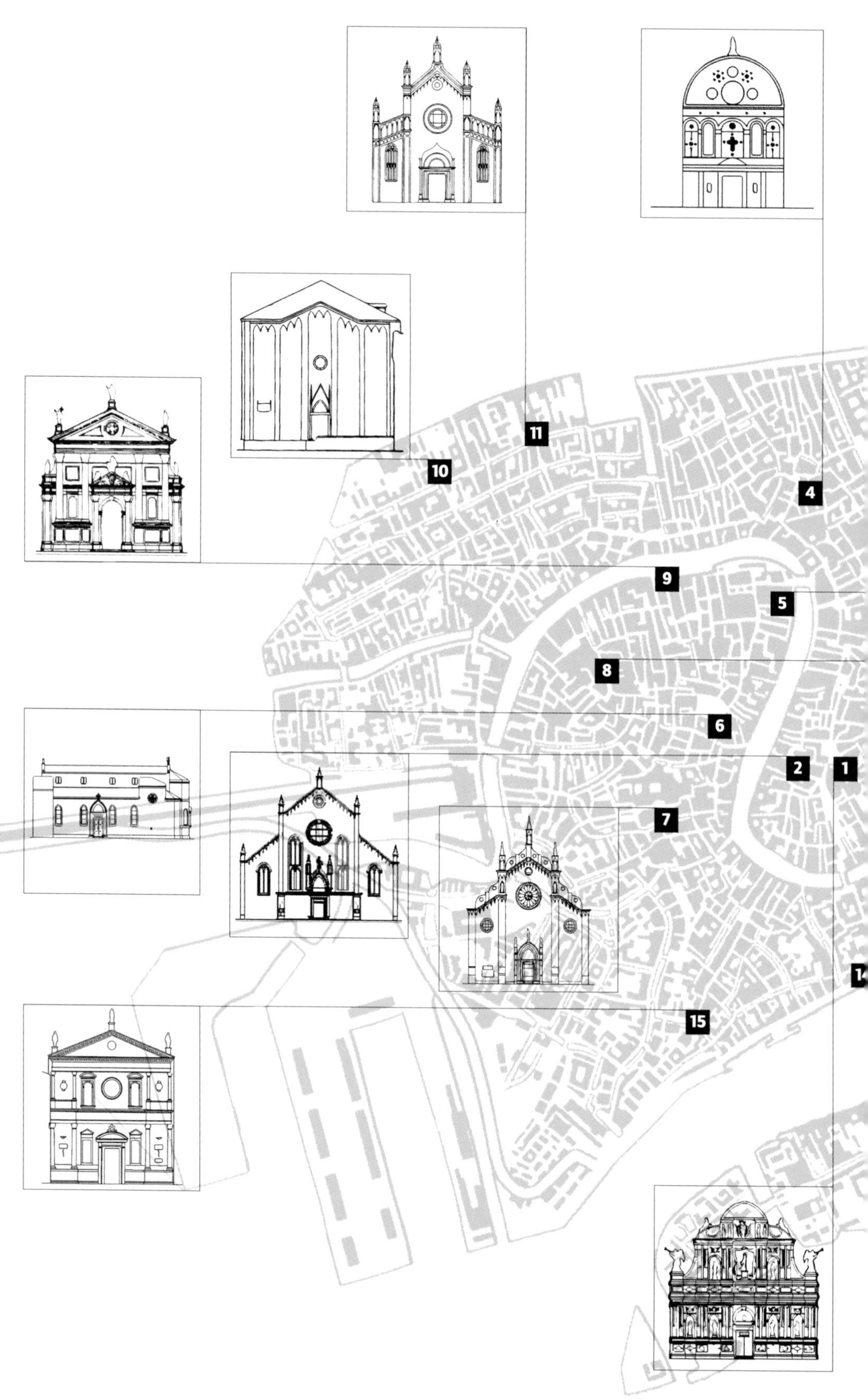

11
4
10
9
5
8
6
2
1
7
15

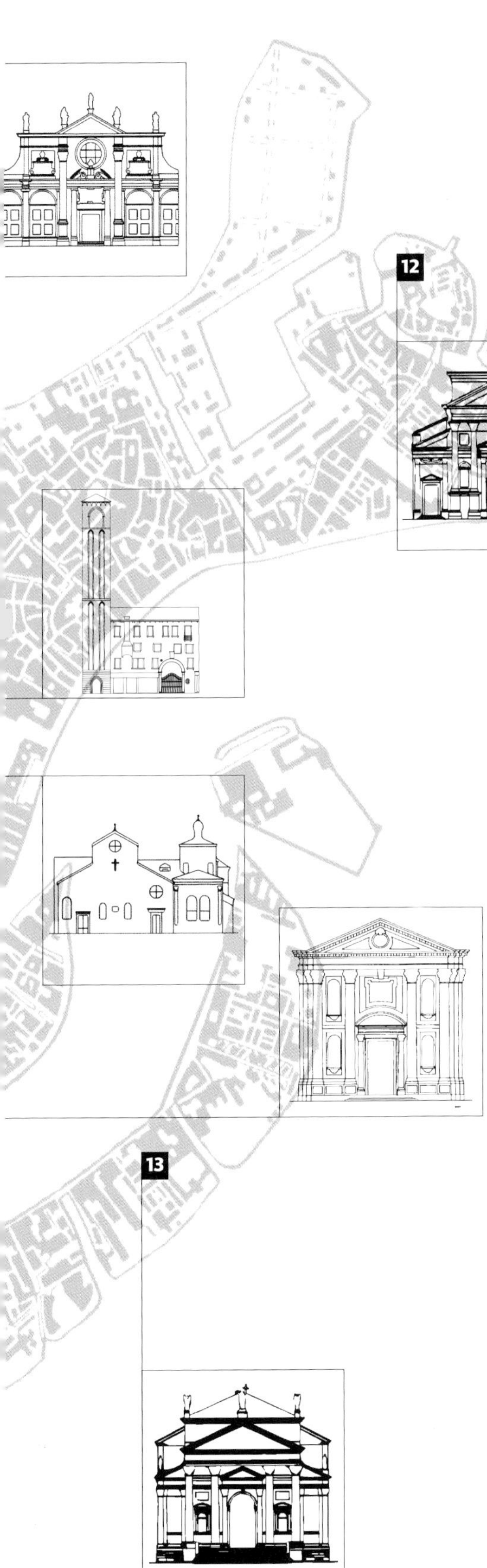

The churches

1 Santa Maria del Giglio

2 Santo Stefano

3 Santa Maria Formosa

4 Santa Maria dei Miracoli

5 San Giovanni Elemosinario

6 San Polo

7 Santa Maria Gloriosa dei Frari

8 San Giacomo dall'Orio

9 San Stae

10 Sant'Alvise

11 Madonna dell'Orto

12 San Pietro di Castello

13 Santissimo Redentore

14 Santa Maria del Rosario (Gesuati)

15 San Sebastiano

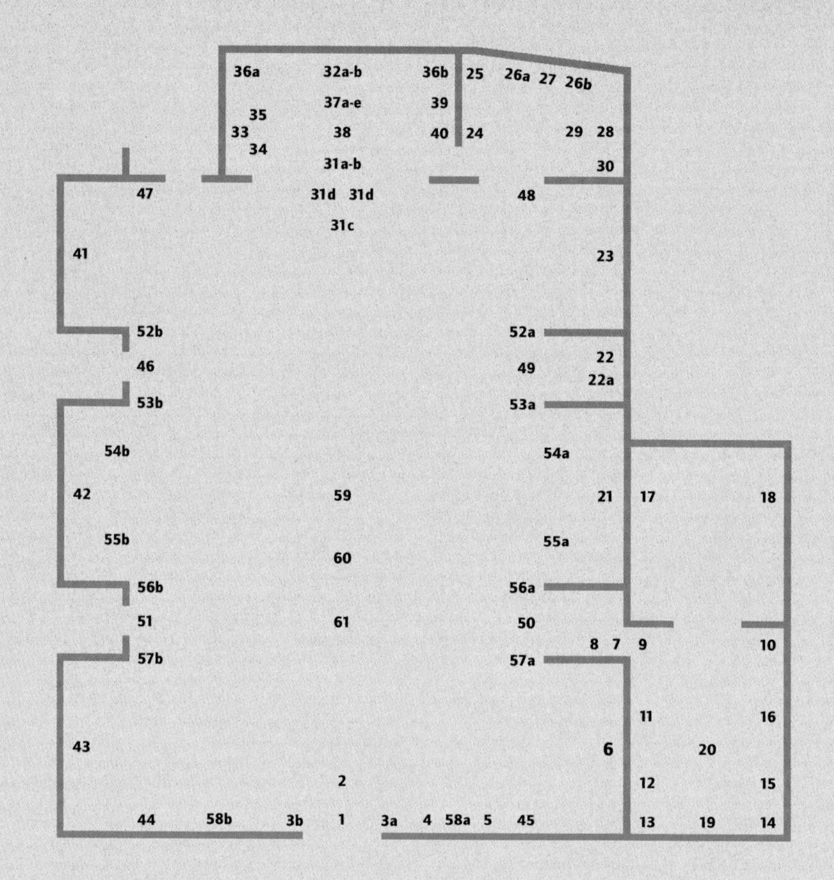
36a 32a-b 36b 25 26a 27 26b
37a-e 39
35
33 38 40 24 29 28
34
31a-b 30
47 31d 31d 48
31c
41 23
52b 52a
22
46 49
22a
53b 53a
54b 54a
42 59 21 17 18
55b 55a
60
56b 56a
51 61 50
8 7 9 10
57b 57a
11 16
43 6 20
2 12 15
44 58b 3b 1 3a 4 58a 5 45 13 19 14

1. Battista del Moro
Consecration of the Baptismal Font, 1562

2. Giulio del Moro
Last Supper, XVI c.

3a-b. Giuseppe Porta called Salviati, *The Four Sibyls (Agrippina, Cumana, Tiburtina, Delfica)*, XVI c.

4. Niccolò di Giovanni Fiorentino, *St Jerome in the Cave*, c. 1468-70

5. Giulio del Moro
Risen Christ, XVI c.

6. Carlo Loth, *Virgin and Child, St Anthony and the Martyrdom of St Eugene* XVII c.

7. MOLIN CHAPEL
Alessandro Vittoria
Bust of Girolamo Molin
XVI c.

8. MOLIN CHAPEL
Giambattista Piazzetta and Giuseppe Angeli
St Vincent Ferrer, 1750

9-10. MOLIN CHAPEL
Anonymous, XVIII c.
- *Christ Redeemer*
- *Death of St Joseph*

11-17. MOLIN CHAPEL
Giovanni Antonio Pellegrini
XVIII c.
- *Deposition in the Sepulchre*
- *Resurrection of Naim*
- *Crowning with Thorns*
- *Christ praying in the Olive Grove*
- *Christ healing the Blind*
- *Flagellation*
- *Ascent to Calvary*

18. MOLIN CHAPEL
Antonio Zanchi
Ulysses recognised by Argo the Dog, XVII c.

19. MOLIN CHAPEL
Peter Paul Rubens
Virgin and Child with the Infant St John, XVII c.

20. CEILING OF THE MOLIN CHAPEL
Domenico Tintoretto (attr.)
Virgin and Child, XVI c.

21. Gian Maria Morlaiter
St Gregorio Barbarigo
XVIII c.

22. BAPTISTRY
Antonio Corradini (attr.)
The Baptist, XVIII c.

22a. BAPTISTRY
Domenico Paternò (attr.)
Stuccoes, 1730

23. Jacopo Negretti called Palma Giovane
Visitation, XVI-XVII c.

24. SACRISTY
Pietro Muttoni called Pietro della Vecchia and Antonio Zanchi
Adoration of the Magi
XVII c.

25. SACRISTY
Veneto-Cretan iconographer
Virgin and Child, XVI c.

26a-b. SACRISTY
Giulio del Moro
Two Angels Praying, XVI c.

27. SACRISTY
Desiderio da Settignano (attr.)
Head of the Infant St John altar frontal, XV c.

28. SACRISTY
Antonio Zanchi, *Abraham teaches Astrology to the Egyptians*, XVII c.

29. SACRISTY
Andrea Meldolla called Schiavone (attr.)
Annunciation, XVI c.

30. SACRISTY
Veneto School, *Adoration of the Sheperds*, XVII c.

31a-b. CHANCEL
Heinrich Meyring
Annunciation, XVII c.

31c-d. CHANCEL
Giovanni Comin, XVII c.
- *Last Supper*, altar frontal
- *Angels with Symbols of the Passion*

32a. CHANCEL
Domenico Ruggia and Michiel Maes, *Wooden dossals, frames, architecture and structure of organ* 1696-98

32b. CHANCEL
Vincenzo Mascioni
Organ, 1913

33. CHANCEL
Alessandro Vittoria
Epitaph of Procurator Giulio Contarini, XVI c.

34. CHANCEL
Circle of Paolo Caliari called Veronese
Virgin and Child, XVI c.

35. CHANCEL
Francesco Solimena
Our Lady of Sorrows, XVII c.

36a-b. CHANCEL
Jacopo Robusti called Tintoretto
The Four Evangelists organ doors, 1552

37a-e. CHANCEL
Antonio Zanchi, 1696-98
Birth of Christ and Musician Angels, Eternal Father with Angels and Cherubs, choir parapet and ceiling

38. CHANCEL
Giuseppe Porta called Salviati
Annunciation, XVI c.

39. CHANCEL
Antonio Zanchi
St Francis of Assisi, XVII c.

40. CHANCEL
Andrea Celesti (attr.)
Holy Family with St Catherine, XVII c.

41. Jacopo Robusti called Tintoretto and workshop
Christ and Saints Francis of Paola and Justine, XVI c.

42. Gian Maria Morlaiter (attr.)
Immacolata, XVIII c.

43. Antonio Zanchi
Martyrdom of St Anthony
XVII c.

44-48. ABOVE THE ENTABLATURE
Antonio Zanchi, XVII c.
- *Consecration of the Church*
- *Virgin Enthroned as Symbol of the Mother Church and the Titular Saints of the Affiliated Churches*
- *Immacolata*
- *Annunciata*
- *Venice in Supplication*

49-51. Giambattista Volpato, XVII c.
- *Descent of the Holy Spirit*
- *Adoration of the Sheperds*
- *Betrothal of the Virgin*

52a-b.
VIA CRUCIS, 1755-56
Francesco Zugno
- *I Station*
- *XIV Station*

53a-b.
VIA CRUCIS, 1755-56
Giambattista Crosato
- *II Station*
- *XIII Station*

54a-b.
VIA CRUCIS, 1755-56
Domenico Maggiotto
- *III Station*
- *XII Station*

55a-b.
VIA CRUCIS, 1755-56
Francesco Fontebasso
- *IV Station*
- *XI Station*

56a-b.
VIA CRUCIS, 1755-56
Giuseppe Angeli
- *V Station*
- *X Station*

57a-b.
VIA CRUCIS, 1755-56
Gaspare Diziani
- *VI Station*
- *IX Station*

58a-b.
VIA CRUCIS, 1755-56
Jacopo Marieschi
- *VII Station*
- *VIII Station*

59-61. CEILING
Antonio Zanchi, 1690-96
- *Birth of the Virgin*
- *Coronation of the Virgin*
- *Assumption of the Virgin*

Façade

The building

The church of Santa Maria del Giglio has a similar history to that of many other Venetian churches, including San Stae. Its very early origins are traditionally traced to the tenth century, when it was laid out in Byzantine basilica style with nave and aisles. The church then underwent several restorations over the centuries before being completely rebuilt in 1680. This resulted in an extremely bright, flat-roofed space marked by three shallow chapels on each side and a slightly deeper chancel which may still be admired. However, unlike San Stae, Santa Maria del Giglio was not rotated on its axis but left in its traditional east-west orientation. Similar to the nearby church of Santo Stefano, one side faces a broad square opening onto the Grand Canal, while the façade overlooks a fairly narrow calle offering the visitor a decidedly foreshortened view.

Details of the façade

The façade

The façade is the main feature of this church. Conceived quite independently of the interior, it is a sensational example of the commemorative façade, where the iconographic rhetoric of noble celebration takes on a rather pompous air. It is also in the style of Veneto art typical of the war of Candia period; a style that seemed committed to anxiously exorcising evil omens and the more actual events linked to Venice's imminent decline.

Antonio Barbaro obtained 'absolute control' over the façade from the Senate and from the church Chapter, after a distinguished military and political career. In his will of 1678 he then left 30,000 ducats and precise instructions on how Giuseppe Sardi was to transform it into a genuine funeral monument to the glory of himself and his family. He died in 1679 and the façade was constructed between 1680 and 1683.

With its powerful play of chiaroscuro, it is composed of one order of Ionic demi-columns, one of Corinthian demi-columns and an attic with open-topped pediment. Six pairs of demi-columns on high plinths in the lower order separate the entrance from four niches housing the statues of Antonio's four brothers: Giovan Maria, Carlo, Francesco and Marino, all clothed according to the public offices they held. The second order is divided by four pairs; in the middle is a statue of Antonio on the sarcophagus framed by a rich marble drape, between Honour, Virtue, Fame and Wisdom. The family coat of arms and numerous allegorical figures are depicted on the attic. The panels on the plinths of the second order are carved with battle scenes, while on the first they carry the city plans of Zara, Candia, Padua, Rome, Corfu and Spalato: all referring to Antonio's military and political triumphs.

Peter Paul Rubens

An extremely valuable work is housed in Santa Maria del Giglio: a *Virgin and Child with the Infant St John* by Rubens, the only painting by this artist in Venice. The central section on paper is by Rubens, and this is fixed onto canvas and connected to a generic background comprising a tree and curtain hanging on the right, by a late seventeenth-century painter probably from the Veneto.

Despite its critical vicissitudes over the centuries, there is no lack of elements substantiating the author of the painting and its very high quality: the brilliant quality of the flesh tones, especially in the children; the emotional intensity of the looks; the material richness and the expert technique evident in the several tones of Titian-style red on which the chromatic distribution of the entire fragment is based. Deep layers of solid and glazed lacquer are superimposed, often tone on tone and finely touched, from the clothes of the Virgin shaded in the grey filaments and earth green of the veil falling on her neck, to the profiles and extremely tender tips of the two children's fingers, heightened in white with the tip of the brush. Then there is the skillful painting of the Virgin's ear and of every other element in the work; the power of invention and of colour evident in the small patch of sky; the effect of shaping on form, seen in the facial features and breast of the Virgin, portrayed to great plastic effect, and partly the entire placement of the figures and overall composition, sensitive to the lessons of Caravaggio.

19. Peter Paul Rubens
Virgin and Child with the Infant St John, XVII c.

36b. Jacopo Robusti called Tintoretto
The Evangelists Luke and Matthew
organ door, 1552

Tintoretto

Tintoretto's *Evangelists* hung in the previous church, commissioned by the procurator Giulio Contarini: one canvas showing Mark and John and the other Luke and Matthew.
These are undoubtedly quite unique works by an artist who generally created crowded, dynamic compositions. At times, however, especially

29. Andrea Meldolla called Schiavone (attr.)
Annunciation, XVI c.

25. Veneto-cretan iconographer
Virgin and Child, XVI c.

in his early years, he paused to contemplate single images, and it was here that the profound nature of his religious spirituality emerged. Confidently resting on clouds like acrobats on a trapeze, the Evangelists are outlined against a golden-brown sky which gives them a dramatic expressiveness. The quite early date sees a Tintoretto pulsating with clever contrasts, drawn in the Romanist manner. Light and colour are blended in the extraordinary atmosphere to characterise the figures not only with their usual symbols (lion, eagle, book and angel), but also revealing a poignant human involvement: the sincere faith Jacopo had in the real importance of the gospels.

Santo Stefano

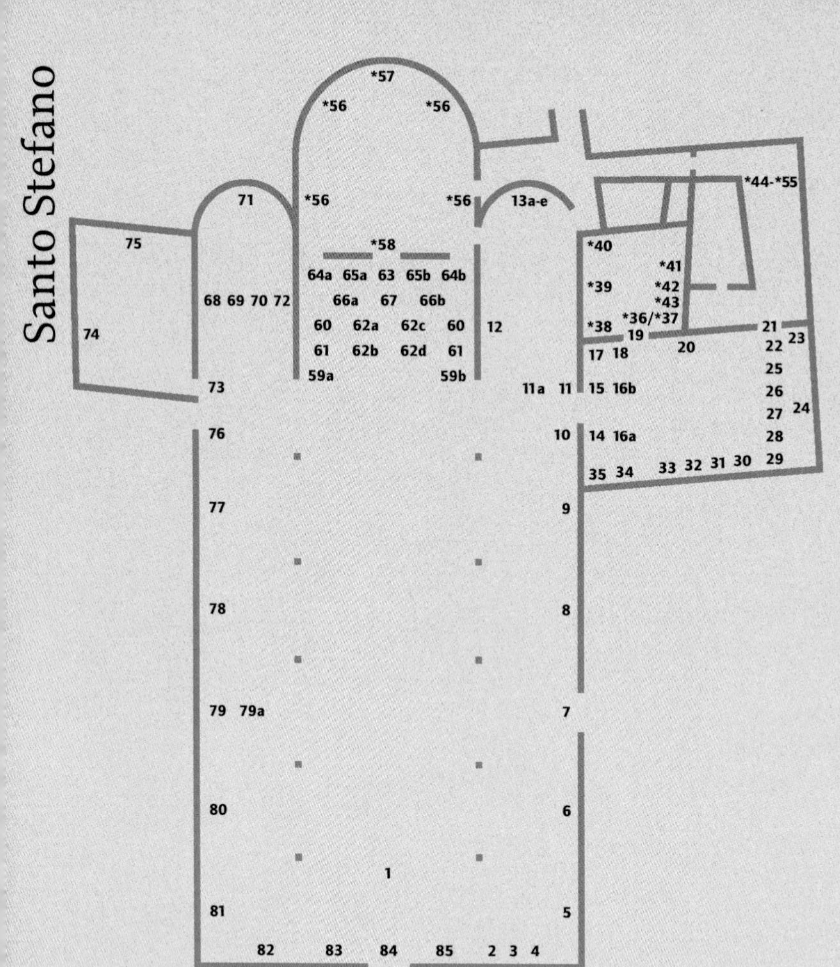

1. Filippo Parodi
Gravestone of the Doge Francesco Morosini, 1694

2. Anonymous, *Urn of Antonio Marcello* († 1555)

3. Anonymous, *Stone to Jacopo dal Verme* († 1408)

4. Anonymous, *Urn of Grazioso Grazioli* († 1558)

5. Nicolò Bambini
Birth of Mary, 1709-12

6. Giuseppe Angeli
St Luigi Gonzaga, St Anthony Abbot an St Francis Xavier
1775

7. Anonymous, *Monument to Pietro Porta* († 1614)

8. Jacopo Marieschi
Virgin with Saints John of Nepomuk and Lucy, c. 1752-55

9. Giustino Menescardi
St Augustine driving out the Heretics, c. 1736-43

10. Giovanni Buora (attr.)
Virgin and Child Enthroned with Saints James the Great and James the Less and the Donors Jacopo and Eugenia Suriano, 1488-93

11. Anonymous, *Monument to Lazzaro Ferro* († 1692)

11a. School of Corbarelli (attr.), *Gravestone of Lazzaro Ferro*, c. 1692

12. Chapel of the Holy Sacrament
Saints Augustine, William, Nicholas of Tolentino and Monica with Angels, c. 1591

13a-e.
Chapel of the Holy Sacrament
Giulio del Moro, 1604-06
- *Tabernacle*
- *Four Angels with Instruments of the Passion*
- *Redeemer and Two Angels*
- *St Peter and St Mark*

behind the tabernacle
- *Dead Christ supported by Angels*

14-16a-b.
Main Sacristy
Gaspare Diziani, 1733
- *Flight into Egypt*
- *Adoration of the Magi*
- *Massacre of the Innocents*

17-18. Main Sacristy
Giovanni Agostino da Lodi, c. 1502-04
- *St John the Baptist and St Jerome*
- *Mystic Marriage of St Catherine*

19. Main Sacristy
Antonio Triva (attr.)
Cardinal Egidio Canisio of Viterbo, 1651-65

20. Main Sacristy
Jacopo Robusti called Tintoretto and assistants
Last Supper, 1579-80

21. Main Sacristy
Antonio Triva (attr.)
Cardinal Girolamo Seripando, 1651-65

22. Main Sacristy
Jacopo Robusti called Tintoretto
Resurrection, c. 1565

23. Main Sacristy
Antonio Triva (attr.)
Pietà, 1651-65

24. Main Sacristy
Sante Peranda
Martyrdom of St Stephen
c. 1630-38

25. Main Sacristy
Anonymous, *Relic niche*, 1621

26. Main Sacristy
Bartolomeo Vivarini
St Nicholas of Bari, c. 1475

27. Main Sacristy
Giuseppe Angeli
Crucifixion, c. 1775

28. Main Sacristy
Bartolomeo Vivarini
St Laurence Martyr, c. 1475

29. Main Sacristy
Anonymous, *Relic niche*, 1621

30. Main Sacristy
Pietro Liberi, *The Trinity with St Augustine and St Clare of Montefalco*, c. 1660

31. Main Sacristy
Antonio Triva (attr.)
Cardinal Anchero Tarcento, 1651-65

32-33. Main Sacristy
Jacopo Robusti called Tintoretto and assistants
1579-80
- *The Washing of the Feet*
- *Christ praying in the Olive Grove*

34. Main Sacristy
Antonio Triva (attr.)
Cardinal Gregorio Petrochino of Montelparo
1651-65

35. Main Sacristy
Bonifacio de' Pitati
Holy Family with St Mary Magdalene and St Catherine
1528-30

***36.** Treasury
Veneto-Tuscan artist
Tabernacle with Two Angels Praying, c. 1430-40

***37.** Treasury
French sculptor
Virgin and Child, c. 1412-20

***38.** Treasury
Bartolomeo Litterini (attr.)
St Nicholas of Tolentino's Miracle of the Arm, c. 1710-20

***39.** Treasury
Liturgical vestments and reliquaries, XII-XIX c.

***40.** Treasury
Coat of Arms of Doge Francesco Morosini
end of XVII c.

***41.** Treasury
Liturgical vestments and reliquaries
XVII-XVIII c.

***42.** Treasury
Liturgical basin, c. 1530

***43.** Treasury
Anonymous, Veneto
St Bartholomew, c. 1780-90

***44-45.**
Cloister of the Sculptures
Jacobello and Pierpaolo dalle Masegne, c. 1390-95
- *St John the Baptist*
- *St Anthony of Padua*

***46-47.**
Cloister of the Sculptures
Pietro Lombardo and assistants, c. 1476-1480
- *St Jerome*
- *St Andrew*

***48.** Cloister of the Sculptures
Tullio Lombardo, *Bust relief of young saint*, c. 1505

***49.** Cloister of the Sculptures
Giovanni Buora (attr.)
Female figure, c. 1490

***50.** Cloister of the Sculptures
Gianmaria Mosca
St John the Baptist, c. 1524-26

***51-52.**
Cloister of the Sculptures
Strasbourg carver
second half of XV c.
- *St Jerome*
- *St Andrew*

***53-54.**
Cloister of the Sculptures
Circle of Lombardo, XV c.
- *Bust of St Nicholas of Bari*
- *Bust of St Nicholas of Tolentino*

***55.** Cloister of the Sculptures
Antonio Canova
Gravestone of Giovanni Falier
1808

***56.** Choir
Leonardo Scalamanzo and Marco da Vicenza
Choir stalls, 1581-88

***57.** Choir
Lombardesque workshop
Remains of doorway to choir, c. 1480, built into wall around door by Gabriele dalla Volta, 1526

***58.** Choir
Vestments, XVI-XIX c.

59a. Chancel
Workshop of Alessandro Vittoria, *Candelabrum*, 1577

59b. Chancel
Anonymous, *Candelabrum*, copy of previous, 1617

60-61. Chancel
Lombardesque workshop
c. 1480
- *Remains of marble choir septo*
- *The Twelve Apostles*

62a-d. Chancel
Giovanni Buora, c. 1480
- *St Nicholas of Tolentino*
- *St Simplicius*
- *St Clare of Montefalco*
- *St Paul First Anchorite*

63. Chancel
Antonio Puzo and Paolo Panizza
Main altar, c. 1620-25

64a-b. Chancel
Lombardesque workshop
XVI century
- *St Stephen*
- *St Augustine*

65a-b. Chancel
Anonymous
Annunciation, XV c.

66a-b. Chancel
Girolamo Campagna (attr.)
XVI c.
- *St Mark*
- *St Clare of Montefalco*

67. Chancel
Benedetto Corbarelli
Martyrdom of St Stephen altar frontal, 1656

68. St Michael's Chapel
Anonymous, *Urn of Giovanni Boldù* († 1537)

69. St Michael's Chapel
Anonymous, *Monument to Marino Zorzi* († 1532)

70. St Michael's Chapel
Style of Pietro Lombardo
St Michael Archangel, c. 1470

71. St Michael's Chapel
Anonymous
St Michael Archangel, XVII c.

72. St Michael's Chapel
Alessandro Vittoria and assistants
Monument to Giovanni Battista Ferretti, 1557

73. Anonymous
St Nicholas of Tolentino, XV c.

74. Baptistry
Giulio del Moro, *Baptismal font with St John the Baptist*, 1592

75. Baptistry
Pomponio Amalteo
Baptism of Christ, XVI c.

76. Baldassarre Longhena and Girolamo Paliari
Monument to Bartolomeo d'Alviano, 1628-33

77. Girolamo Brusaferro,
Virgin and Child with Saints Mark, Phocas and Peter, 1737

78. Antonio Foler
Martyrdom of St Stephen
XVI-XVII c.

79. Circle of Jacopo Robusti called Tintoretto
Coronation of the Virgin, XVI c. with eighteenth-century additions

79a. Pietro Lombardo and assistants, *St Nicholas of Tolentino*, c. 1475-80

80. Teodoro Matteini
Lament over Christ descended from the Cross, XIX c.

81. Leonardo Corona
Madonna of the Belt with Saints Augustine, Monica, Stephen, Nicholas of Tolentino and William of Aquitaine
c. 1591-95

82. Giovanni Battista Groppelli (attr.)
Virgin and Child, XVII c.

83. Giovanni Buora (attr.)
Monument to Jacopo Suriano
1488-93

84. Anonymous
Equestrian monument to Domenico Contarini, 1644-50

85. Workshop of Alessandro Vittoria, *Monument to Antonio Zorzi* (†1588)

Origins

The conventual church was founded in 1294 by the Augustinian hermits of Sant'Anna di Castello, who had been in Venice since 1240. They named it after Saints Augustine and Stephen, the former being the inspiration of their order; the latter because Augustine himself had declared a personal devotion to Saint Stephen. He had devoted the longest chapter of his *City of God* to this first martyr, as an exemplary figure of the original Jerusalem community. The dedication expresses the active and historical role of the charity in a community that maintained its hermit image, but chose to establish itself in the central part of the city. This was in line with the other Augustinian orders coming to Venice, at a time when the peripheral areas were being taken up by the big churches of the mendicant orders. It seems that work was not completed until early 1325, to then be taken up again with a vengeance at the beginning of the fifteenth century. The original nave and aisle structure was retained, but the chancel section was extended out over the rio del Santissimo on an audacious platform that still supports the main apse. The church thus became one of the finest examples of Venetian flamboyant Gothic.

32. Jacopo Robusti called Tintoretto and assistants
The Washing of the Feet, 1579-80
detail

Exterior

Though rather imposing, the building is not of any particular urbanistic importance in relation to the *campo* faced by its right side, while the façade is somewhat diminished by looking onto a *calle* quite out of proportion to its significant size, allowing only a restricted view. The façade reflects the internal tripartition, having a higher and wider central section enriched with Gothic elements. These include a superb doorway decorated with roping, bands of vegetal volutes and leaves alongside, an ogee arch with a web of three-lobed lunettes between two lateral pilasters and a rich motif of leaves enclosing an angel and supporting a God the Father at the top.

Interior

The interior is vast and bright, already suggesting a Renaissance sense of space: the nave and aisles ending in apsidal chapels are separated by large ogee spans, supported on columns of white Greek and red Verona marble, alternated longitudinally and crosswise, with differently painted capitals. The nave is frescoed in the same diamond pattern of red and white bricks as that used to decorate the Ducal Palace. The extrados' of the arches take up the curling leaf frieze of the doorway in monochrome, here supporting half statues of Augustinian saints.

The five-lobed, wooden keel roof resembles wind-filled sails and is particularly striking. Painted and richly decorated with rosettes and lacunars, it is comparable to those of San Giacomo dall'Orio and San Polo, or to that of the Eremitani church in Padua.

26. Bartolomeo Vivarini
St Nicholas of Bari, c. 1475

28. Bartolomeo Vivarini
St Laurence Martyr, c. 1475

20. Jacopo Robusti called Tintoretto and assistants
Last Supper, 1579-80

33. Jacopo Robusti called Tintoretto and assistants
Christ praying in the Olive Grove, 1579-80

The present altars are from the first half of the eighteenth century, while the main altar, a masterpiece of Venetian Baroque, and the arrangement of the chancel, date from the early seventeenth century.

The sacristies and sculptures cloister

There are several works of great value in the main sacristy, including four canvases by Jacopo Tintoretto and workshop: a small *Resurrection*, of circa 1565, and three large works of 1579-80: the *Last Supper, The Washing of the Feet* and *Christ praying in the Olive Grove*. These reveal the sixteenth-century artist's passion for grandiose, showy, restless compositions and for the bold foreshortening of figures within architectural scenes, where all possible contrasts of light and shade are used to identify and underline the movement of the figures, achieving effects of great dramatic suggestion. The artist's phantasmagorical and visionary tendencies are accentuated in his late works, such as these, alongside a tone of greater narrative humility and more intimate spiritual meditation. A variety of liturgical objects and holy jewellery of diverse origins and centuries is collected in the smaller sacristy, while the church's sculptural works are exhibited in the adjacent cloister, including pieces by Pietro Lombardo and Giovanni Falier's tombstone. The latter is a neo-Classical work by Antonio Canova, created as a tribute to the patron of his first works. It remained in the sculptor's Rome studio until his death in 1822, when it was brought to Venice; it was then taken to the Villa Falier in Asolo and finally, in 1956, brought here to the church of Santo Stefano.

The choir

As in many convent churches, the choir was probably originally in the second bay of the central nave in front of the chancel. It comprised wooden stalls within a marble septo, possibly a transition work by Antonio Gambello, decorated with reliefs and sculptures, probably by Giovanni Buora, similar to one of the few remaining examples: that in the Frari. The structure was dismantled in about 1613, according to the requirements of the Council of Trent, with the stalls being partially recomposed in the main altar and two façades of the septo arbitrarily set in the walls of the chancel.

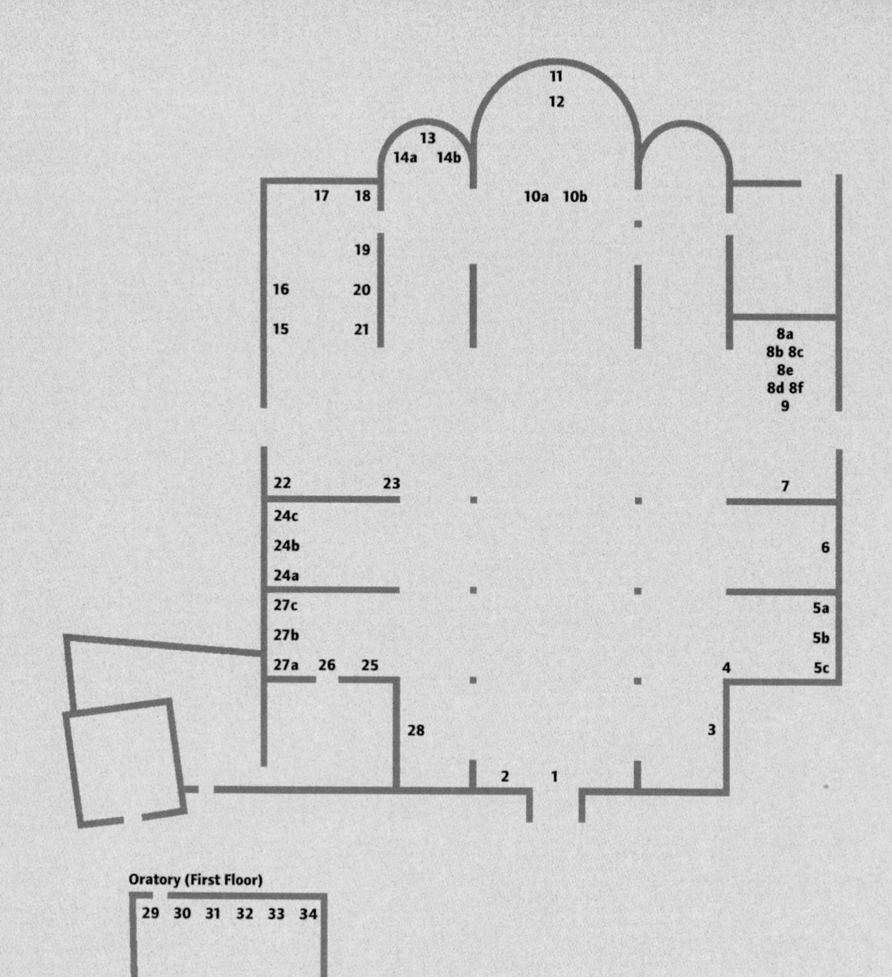
11
12
13
14a 14b
17 18
10a 10b
19
16 20
15 21
8a
8b 8c
8e
8d 8f
9
22 23
7
24c
24b
6
24a
27c
5a
27b
5b
27a 26 25
4
5c
28
3
2 1
Oratory (First Floor)
29 30 31 32 33 34

1. Pasquale Ferrari
Organ, under construction

2. Veneto-cretan School
Our Lady of Consolation or of Lepanto, pre 1571

3. Vincenzo Catena (attr.)
Circumcision of Jesus, XVI c.

4. Lazzaro Bastiani (attr.), *God the Father and Angels*, XV c.

5a-c. Bartolomeo Vivarini, 1473
- *Meeting of Joachim and Anne*
- *Our Lady of Mercy*
- *Birth of the Virgin*

6. Jacopo Negretti called Palma Giovane
Madonna 'in pietà' and St Francis of Assisi, post 1604?

7. Leandro Bassano
Last Supper, XVI c.

8a-f. Jacopo Negretti called Palma Vecchio, c. 1523
- *Dead Christ supported by Mary*
- *St John the Baptist*
- *St Vincent Ferrer*
- *St Sebastian*
- *St Barbara*
- *St Anthony Abbot*

9. Giuseppe Torretti
Martyrdom of St Barbara altar frontal, 1719

10a-b. Veneto sculptor XVII century
- *St Paul*
- *St Dominic*

11. Giulia Lama
The Virgin and Saints Mark and Magno, c. 1710

12. Giovanni Segala (attr.)
Presentation to the Doge of the Brides kidnapped by Narentine Pirates, XVII c.

13. Venetian School
Our Lady of the Birth, XVI c.

14a-b.
Venetian sculptor, XVII c.
- *St Matthew the Apostle*
- *St James the Apostle*

15. Circle of Pietro Negri
Christ descended and lamented by Mary, Mary Magdalene and St John, XVII c.

16. Circle of Pietro Liberi
Mary Magdalene oiling Christ's Feet in Simon's House, XVII c.

17. Giulio del Moro
Christ Redeemer, XVI c.

18. Circle of Ermanno Stroiffi
St Anthony, XVII c.

19. Veneto School
Presentation of Jesus at the Temple, XVI c.

20. Veneto School
The Trinity, XVIII c.

21. Antonio Foler
Birth of the Virgin, XVI c.

22. Baldassarre d'Anna
Approval of the Order of the Blessed Trinity, 1619

23. Lattanzio Querena
Virgin and Child, copy after Sassoferrato, XIX c.

24a-c. Antonio Ermolao Paoletti, c. 1890
- *St Luigi Gonzaga*
- *St Simeon indicating Jesus*
- *St Anthony of Padua*

25. Venetian School
Christ's Capture in the Garden XVI c.

26. Venetian School
St Marcellinus, XVI c.

27a-c.-28.
Lattanzio Querena, c. 1830
- *St Vincent*
- *The Sacred Heart, St Alphonsus Liguori and St Luigi Gonzaga*
- *St Peter*
- *Holy Virgin Marina*

29. Oratory (First Floor)
Giandomenico Tiepolo
Virgin and Child, c. 1760

30. Oratory (First Floor)
Paolo Pagani (attr.)
St Peter the Apostle, XVIII c.

31. Oratory (First Floor)
Giambettino Cignaroli
Madonna, c. 1750

32. Oratory (First Floor)
Giovanni Battista Salvi called Sassoferrato
Virgin and Child, XVII c.

33. Oratory (First Floor)
Pietro da Messina
Madonna, XV c.

34. Oratory (First Floor)
Early imitator of Giorgione
Christ carrying the Cross, XVI c.

Origins

The first church on this site is believed to date from as early as the seventh century, when the Virgin is said to have appeared in a vision to St Magno, the bishop of Oderzo, telling him where to build a church dedicated to her. The building obviously underwent various restoration works, particularly in the ninth and twelfth centuries, eventually taking on a Byzantine, Greek cross shape with central dome, similar to the *cuba di mezzo* (dome) in St Mark's. The façade looked onto the canal, with churchyard in front that was almost isolated in the large *campo* but whose left side faced the more open part; an arrangement very similar to that of San Giacomo dall'Orio.

8a-f. Jacopo Negretti called Palma Vecchio
Polyptych of St Barbara, c. 1523
detail

The new church

With the old church virtually in ruins, at the end of sixteenth century it was decided to completely reconstruct the building; the work was entrusted to Mauro Codussi from Bergamo and began in 1492. Codussi had been working in Venice for over twenty years and had begun experimenting with the new proto-Renaissance language, working on the construction of San Michele in Isola, San Pietro di Castello and San Zaccaria – all churches with a basilica nave and aisle layout. In this case his work on the typically Byzantine, Greek cross shape entailed an adaptation to a nave and side aisle Latin cross with transept. But it was carried out in a rather veiled manner: it is certainly possible to read the Latin cross in the layout, with quite deep lateral and apsidal chapels, but Greek cross proportions remain in the almost square perimeter. As may be understood, it was a very complex plan which created rather particular spatiality. Entering from the main doorway, the church opens up in all directions, in width, in height and in depth. Codussi imposed a very powerful hierarchy of space, also assisted by the clear hierarchy of light, while the severity and purity of the whole are accentuated by the whiteness of the surfaces, broken only – in Brunelleschi fashion – by the grey of the structural stone. The deep, barrel-vaulted side chapels communicate via unusual biforate openings with small central column; the cross-vaulted nave is as wide as the chapels are deep. The aisles comprise a series of squares with sides measuring half of the nave width and are roofed with small domes on pendentives, six in total, which in section have a height between that of the central nave and the aisles. The highest point is the dome on circular drum at the meeting of nave and transept, also cross vaulted, as are the apsidal chapels. All adding up to a spatial arrangement that is quite worthy of a Renaissance architect.

The façades

When Codussi died in 1504, he had still not begun work on the façades, which long remained unfinished. In 1542 the Cappello family financed construction of the façade towards the *rio* as a funerary monument to themselves, by an unknown architect.

The rigid, solemn façade is divided into three by panelled Corinthian pilasters on high pedestals, supporting a bossed entablature crowned with a full-width, triangular pediment carrying the family coat of arms. Returned Ionic columns frame the doorway – whose Greek marble jambs are from the twelfth century church – and support a funerary urn with maritime decorations on which stands the imperious statue of *capitano generale da mar* Vincenzo Cappello, who died in 1541, sculpted in Roman military uniform by Domenico di Pietro Grazioli da Salò. The north façade was financed by the same Cappello family and also constructed by an unknown architect, but was not completed until 1604. It is divided into five sections by panelled Corinthian pilasters on high pedestals and plain, returned Ionic lesenes; the central section, corresponding to the head of the transept, is highlighted by the doorway, the Ionic demi-columns, the rose window and the tympanum. There are

Interior

busts of three members of the Cappello family, including Senator Vincenzo who died in 1604, on the upper order.

Tryptych of Our Lady of Mercy

The first chapel on the right holds one of the finest masterpieces of the Murano artist Bartolomeo Vivarini, signed and dated 1473. The tryptych on panel in marble frame shows *Our Lady of Mercy* in the centre, the *Meeting of Joachim and Anne* on the left and the *Birth of the Virgin* on the right. Painted in tempera, it clearly shows the Mantegna and earlier Squarcione influence on the art produced in Vivarini's workshop – regarded as the second most important in Venice after that of the Bellini at the dawn of the Renaissance. A long way from the tonalism of Bellini, Vivarini focused this entire work on the development of a sharp, almost sculptural line – which harmonises well with the marble frame – enhanced by colouring that is brilliant, almost glassy, to the point of suggesting a not negligible influence by the work of Donatello who was at that time working in Venice on his Baptist for the church of the Frari and in Padua.

Palma Vecchio

The big altar polyptych in the Scuola dei Bombardieri, one of the artist's more significant works, shows Saints John the Baptist, Vincent Ferrer, Sebastian and Anthony Abbot gathered around Saint Barbara, surmounted by a dramatic *Pietà*. At this time under Titian's protective wing, Palma transferred all his impressive consistency into the figure of the saint, cloaked in a red garment that highlights her blonde magnificence as if in a portrait from life. The marble frame by Giuseppe Torretti dates from 1719, but the bright colours of the paintings would certainly have been better enhanced by the original in gilt wood.

5a-c. Bartolomeo Vivarini
Tryptych of Our Lady of Mercy
1473

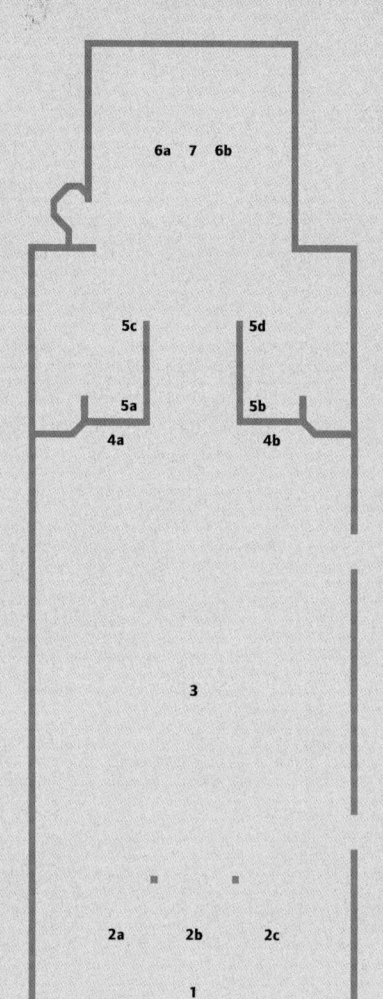

1. Annibale Pugina
Organ, 1919

2a-c. Barco Ceiling
Veneto mannerist, XVI-XVII c.
- *St Francis*
- *Virgin and Child*
- *St Clare*

3. Lacunar Ceiling
Pier Maria Pennacchi (attr.), Vincenzo da Treviso called Dai Destri (attr.), Domenico Caprioli (attr.) and others
Busts of saints and prophets
1528

4a-b. Girolamo Campagna
XVI-XVII c.
- *St Francis*
- *St Clare*

5a-d. Tullio Lombardo
XV-XVI c.
- *St Francis*
- *St Clare*
- *The Archangel Gabriel*
- *Annunciata*

6a-b. Alessandro Vittoria
XVI-XVII c.
- *St Peter*
- *St Anthony Abbot*

7. Nicolò di Pietro (attr.)
Virgin and Child, 1408

Façade and rio side

Chancel

Venice and the Renaissance

Santa Maria dei Miracoli is a very special church, both in historical and artistic terms. It is a votive temple which was designed, built and decorated by a single artist and his workshop, possibly all at the same time, or in two almost concurrent stages. And, erected much more recently than almost all the other churches in Venice, it has survived almost intact. It is located not far from Santa Maria Formosa, which represents the first example of Renaissance architecture in a still fundamentally Gothic Venice, in Codussi's interpretation of the new style. Santa Maria dei Miracoli, on the other hand, is Renaissance according to the Lombardesque school of Pietro Lombardo and his sons. The two churches show how differently the Renaissance was interpreted in Venice by the two Lombards: in one case focusing on spatiality and pure structure, in the other on decoration and the 'skin' of the building – two versions that are perhaps theoretically complementary.

The building

Francesco Amadi commissioned a *Virgin and Child* from Nicolò di Pietro in 1408, which Angelo Amadi then placed outside his houses. It quickly became the object of intense public devotion as it was regarded as having miraculous powers. So in order to give it more fitting surroundings, a group of houses was bought and demolished to make way for a wooden chapel for the image. The Lombardos then completed the new church between 1481 and 1489.
The cleared area was almost rectangular, quite small and lapped by a *rio* from which the left side of the temple rises. It has a single, barrel vaulted nave with almost square, domed apsidale chapel, a nun's gallery against the entrance wall, supported by two small, elegant, sculpted pillars, and a solemn chancel raised on a crypt-sacristy, reached by a wide central stairway flanked by side apses with ambo.
The result may be defined as a precious treasure chest: by its shape, by the dimensions in proportion to most other churches and by the precious nature of the overall decoration. Almost born of a kind of *horror vacui ante litteram*, it is exquisite, unique, a real jewel.

Exterior

The exterior is entirely surrounded by a double order of lesenes: the lower ones are Corinthian and support a plain entablature, while the second order is Ionic with arches above (this is quite contrary to the classical rule governing the hierarchy of orders: from the bottom up these should be first Doric or Tuscan, then Ionic, Corinthian and Composite; in other words they should gradually pass from the 'heavier', more robust, virile orders to the 'lighter', more elegant, feminine ones).

The pedestal plinths of the Corinthian lesenes on the left side rest on strong brackets which are also Ionic. These are lapped by or often beneath the water of the rio, almost as if they were the capitals of a third, lower, submerged order.

The intercolumniations are encrusted with coloured marbles in geometrical figures such as crosses, circles and octagons, and small reliefs; some of the arches have openings showing some ingenuousness, such as the 'squinting' windows of the apse, internally perfect but off-centre outside. The barrel vaulting ends in a semi-circular pediment enclosing a trick of eyes: open in window and blind in coloured marble. The whole is absolutly balanced and quite compact, including the small octagonal bell tower embedded between apse and nave.

Interior

The interior is a real blaze of decoration, coloured marbles, reliefs and sculptures. Every embellishment is exceptionally crafted and rich in shape and invention in an inexhaustible variety of detail. Paintings of the Titian school on the ceiling of the *barco* (nun's gallery) are framed with gilt, inlaid wooden lacunars.

The vault is also divided into lacunars with early sixteenth century paintings of saint and prophets.

7. Nicolò di Pietro (attr.)
Virgin and Child, 1408

Interior

San Giovanni Elemosinario

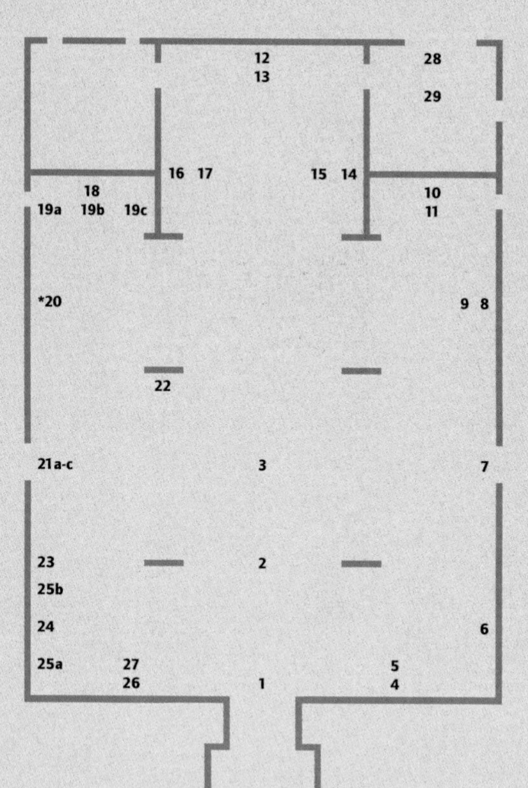

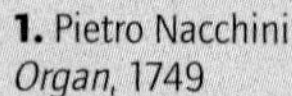

1. Pietro Nacchini
Organ, 1749

2. Anonymous, *Tomb with frescoes*, XVI c.

3. Dome frescoes
Giovanni Antonio de' Sacchis called Pordenone
God Benedictory and Glory of Angels, 1531

4-5. Leonardo Corona
XVI-XVII c.
- *The Investiture of St Nicholas of Bari as Bishop*
- *St Andrew raised on the Cross*

6. Luigi Zandomeneghi
Virgin and Child, 1834

7. Leonardo Corona
The Fall of Manna, 1590

8-9. Jacopo Negretti called Palma Giovane
- *St Roch healing the Plague Victims*, c. 1590
- *Martyrdom of St Catherine of Alexandria*, 1595-99

10. Domenico Tintoretto
St Catherine attended by Angels, XVI-XVII c.

11. Giovanni Antonio de' Sacchis called Pordenone
Saints Catherine, Sebastian and Roch, c. 1532-33

12. Leonardo Corona
Resurrection of Christ, XVI c.

13. Tiziano Vecellio
St John the Almsgiver
1545-50

14-16. Leonardo Corona
XVI c.
- *Moses striking Water from the Rock*
- *Crucifixion of Christ*
- *Christ praying in the Olive Grove*

17. Antonio Vassillacchi called Aliense, *The Washing of the Feet*, XVI c.

18. Leonardo Corona
Ascent to Calvary, XVI c.

19a-c. Anonymous, Veneto
1705
- *St John the Almsgiver*
- *Pietà*
- *St Francis of Assisi*

*** 20.** Jacopo Negretti called Palma Giovane
Heraclius takes the Cross to Jerusalem, c. 1590

21a-c. Marco Vecellio
XVII c.
- *St Mark*
- *The Vicar Gianmaria Carnonali gives the Holy Water to Doge Leonardo Donà*
- *St John the Almsgiver*

22. *Stone in memory of Paolo della Pergola* († 1455)

23. Anonymous
Scenes from the Birth of Christ
VI-VII c.

24. Anonymous, Veneto
Death of Joseph, XVIII c.

25a-b. School of Leonardo Corona, XVI-XVII c.
- *The Archangel Gabriel*
- *Virgin Annunciata*

26. Domenico Tintoretto
The Eternal Father in Glory with Doge Marino Grimani, Dogaressa Morosina Morosini and members of the Scuola dei Pollaioli
XVI-XVII c.

27. Carlo Ridolfi, *Adoration of the Magi*, XVII-XVIII c.

28. Sacristy
Giambattista Pittoni
Virgin and Child with St Philip Neri, c. 1720

29. Sacristy Ceiling
Giambattista Pittoni
St Augustine in Glory
c. 1717-20

The building

Nothing is known about the establishment of the original church of San Giovanni Elemosinario. However, it is certainly very old, given that the earliest documents to have come down to us refer to the collapse of its bell-tower in 1071. This was subsequently rebuilt twice, the second time between 1398 and 1401 in the late-Gothic style still visible today. The present building, completely incorporated into its dense urban setting, was probably rebuilt within the year 1531, after the terrible fire of 1514. This had completely destroyed and devastated the *insula* of Rialto – always a market area – where traffic, shops and financial activities were concentrated. The fire had caused enormous economic damage not only in terms of buildings destroyed, but especially the huge quantity of goods lost. Following that disastrous event, the Senate of the Republic commissioned Antonio Abbondi called Scarpagnino, then working on reconstruction of the east wing of the ducal palace, to completely redesign the whole area with all speed according to criteria of safety, efficiency and order. Scarpagnino worked mainly, but not only, on the so-called *Fabbriche Vecchie*, the porticoed buildings with shops to the left of the Rialto bridge, within which the church was inserted. It is therefore quite probable that he also rebuilt the church itself, keeping the same arched structure of the porticoes for the main doorway and thereby demonstrating the close connection between the buildings. A stone inside the church documents the direct involvement of Doge Andrea Gritti in its reconstruction, meaning it was built as a tribute from the doge: both the simple, modest structure of the church and the way in which reconstruction of the area was carried out, based primarily on practicality, were the direct result of his involvement. The small church is laid out in the form of a Greek cross inscribed in a square, with vaulted ceiling and central conch dome. The chancel, also square, is raised on the crypt, with two small apsidal chapels completing the structure.

The merchant's church

The history of art in Venice is everywhere closely connected to the history of the powerful art and trade fraternities. This is nowhere more important and visible than in San Giovanni Elemosinario. Many guilds were based in the small church at the heart of the market, and these frequently contributed to the decoration of the church itself. Indeed, thanks to these wealthy merchants, the interior of the church is as rich as the outside is simple, essential and classically Renaissance. Not all

23. Anonymous
Scenes from the Birth of Christ
VI-VII c.

the works currently housed there are originals, but many of these are still in place as testimony to such customs.
The ancient school of the *gallineri* (poulterers) had an altar here – the first on the left – from 1597, thanks to the concession of Doge Marino Grimani which is recorded by a stone in the floor in front of it. The *gallineri* guild placed itself under the auspices of the Annunciation of the Blessed Virgin and, at the sides of the altar, there are two panels representing the *Annunciation*. On the left side of the altar, on the entrance wall, a lunette painted by Domenico Tintoretto portrays Doge Marino Grimani and Dogaressa Morosina Morosini worshipping the Holy Father with Members of the Gallineri Guild: recognition of the generous concession of an altar inside the ducal church.

3. Giovanni Antonio de' Sacchis called Pordenone
God Benedictory and Glory of Angels, 1531

The first altar on the right was rather that of the *biavaroli* (fodder merchants): in this case, too, a stone in the floor records the concession by Doge Lodovico Manin in 1792.
The altar to the right of the main altar belonged to the *corrieri* (messengers) whose patron saints were St Catherine of Alexandria and St Roch. The school of the *corrieri* commissioned various paintings representing their patron saints, beginning with the most famous, by Pordenone, depicting *Saints Catherine, Sebastian and Roch*, on the altar. The lunette above this, painted by Domenico Tintoretto, also shows St Catherine, this time tended by angels, as does the big painting on the right wall next to the altar, recounting her martyrdom by sword, painted by Jacopo Palma Giovane. Above this there is another lunette, also by Palma Giovane, portraying *St Roch healing the Plague Victims*.

Pordenone and Titian: a competition between greats?

The church has two extraordinary pictorial documents of two great sixteenth-century artists: Titian and Pordenone. The altarpiece on the main altar by Titian, depicting *St John the Almsgiver*, and the other already mentioned by Pordenone with *Saints Catherine, Sebastian and Roch* on the altar of the *corrieri* were, according to Vasari, the result of a test of skill. Pordenone is supposed to have been encouraged by some noble Venetians who supported him to challenge Titian who had just completed the altarpiece portraying the church's titular saint. At which, on returning to Venice after a trip to Bologna and finding Pordenone to be all the rage in the city with a new painting in direct competition with one of his own, Titian is said to have been extremely

11. Giovanni Antonio de' Sacchis called Pordenone
Saints Catherine, Sebastian and Roch, c. 1532-33

irked. This was not actually the case; it was probably quite the contrary. Indeed, it is legitimate to date Pordenone's altarpiece at around 1533, according to stylistic criteria, while that of Titian probably dates from around 1545-50.

Pordenone presents the titular saints of the *corrieri* in an exquisitely Mannerist composition: the rotary movement of St Sebastian, following the arched shape of the canvas and of the composition itself, the absence of any Naturalist reference and the expansion of the forms are all aspects of the new 'modern' manner which, already in vogue in the rest of Italy, was beginning to also be accepted in Venice in those years. The altarpiece was painted after a long journey to Emilia Romagna where Pordenone had met Parmigianino and Correggio, who undoubtedly influenced him. Despite this, the figures are described in all their physical presence, through the use of full, dark tones and skilful shading, in a synthesis of Venetian Classicism and Mannerism.

9. Jacopo Negretti called Palma Giovane
Martyrdom of St Catherine of Alexandria, c. 1595-99
detail

Titian's *St John the Almsgiver*, on the contrary, stands out with its balance and composure, although the composition is still of Mannerist inspiration, with the figures clearly arranged on a diagonal – from the beggar at bottom left through the saint with open arms to the tip of the astylar cross held by the young assistant. The complex structure of the composition is resolved, however, in the fascinating use of light and in the warm, silky, atmospheric colour. The old saint with his flowing white beard is captured giving alms to the poor, while in the other hand he holds an open book from which he has been reading. The bright, white clothing, tending towards the grey, contrasts powerfully with the dark red of his cloak, attracting the attention. In this moment, Titian is about to overcome his 'Mannerist crisis' and enter the period of his old age, or of his so-called 'magic impressionism', during which his vision of reality seems tinged by a deep unrest. Despite the greater emphasis on colour over design, the brushwork seems to now dissolve in light, and the relation between the colours becomes vibrant and atmospheric.

13. Tiziano Vecellio
St John the Almsgiver, 1545-50

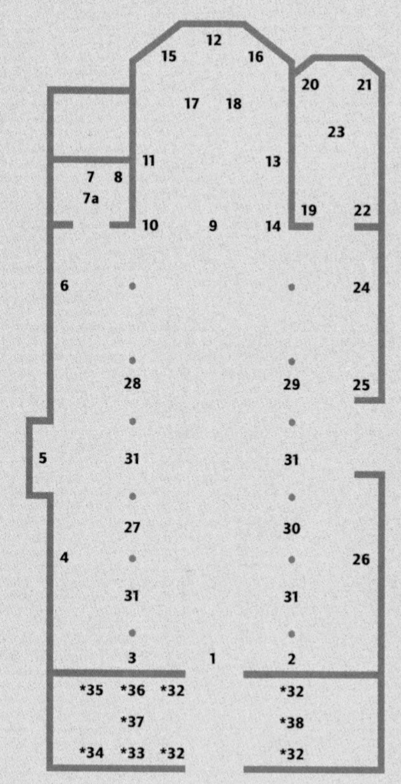

1. Gaetano Callido
Organ, 1763

2. Jacopo Robusti
called Tintoretto
Last Supper, 1568-69

3. Paolo Piazza
St Silvester baptises the Emperor Constantine
XVII c.

4. Jacopo Guarana
The Sacred Heart of Jesus
1802

5. Giambattista Tiepolo
The Virgin appears to St John of Nepomuk, 1754

6. Paolo Piazza
The Preaching of St Paul
XVII c.

7. Paolo Caliari
called Veronese
Betrothal of the Virgin and Angels, c. 1580

7a. Anonymous
Madonna of Loreto, XV c.

8. Anonymous
St Peter, XVIII c.

9. Chancel
Anonymous, *Crucifix*, XIV c.

10-14. Chancel
Jacopo Negretti
called Palma Giovane
- *Consigning the Keys to St Peter*, 1625
- *St Peter sends St Mark to preach the Gospel in Aquileia*, 1625
- *Conversion of St Paul* 1595-1600
- *Temptation of St Anthony Abbot*, c. 1600
- *Liberation of St Anthony Abbot*, c. 1600

15. Chancel
Anonymous
St Paul's Standard, XV c.

16. Chancel
School of Bonifacio de' Pitati
St Laurence amongst the Worshippers, XVI c.

17-18. Chancel
Alessandro Vittoria, XVI c.
- *St Paul*
- *St Anthony Abbot*

19-22. Chapel of the Holy Sacrament
Giuseppe Porta
called Salviati, XVIII c.
- *Ascent to Calvary*
- *Deposition*
- *Christ in the Olive Grove*
- *The Washing of the Feet*

23. Frescoes on vault of Chapel of the Holy Sacrament
Gioacchino Pozzoli
Glory of the Angels and Stories from the Old Testament, XVIII c.

24. Pietro Zandomeneghi
(attr.), *Virgin and Child*, XIX c.

25. Anonymous
Nativity, XVI c.

26. Workshop of Jacopo Robusti called Tintoretto
The Virgin and Saints, XVI c.

27-31. Nave
Anonymous, XIX c.
- *Mark the Evangelist*
- *Luke the Evangelist*
- *Matthew the Evangelist*
- *John the Evangelist*
- *Stories from the Life of St Paul*

***32-*36.** Oratory of the Crucifix
Giandomenico Tiepolo
1747-49
- *Via Crucis*
- *St Philip Neri*
- *St John of Nepomuk*
- *Saints Helena and Macarius*
- *St Vincent Ferrer*

***37-*38.** Ceiling of the Oratory of the Crucifix
Giandomenico Tiepolo
1747-49
- *Glory of the Angels*
- *Resurrection of Christ*

The building

The foundation of a church dedicated to the apostle Paul on the island of San Polo dates from the beginning of the ninth century. The original church has never been radically rebuilt, but has over the centuries undergone extensive rearrangements. The layout and general design is of Byzantine derivation, as are a certain internal spatiality, the two lancet windows in the façade and the fragments of frames and small pillars beside the doorway.
The second layer was a Gothic one, added between the fourteenth and fifteenth centuries. This may be mainly seen in the big, ogee side doorway, slightly splayed and decorated with spiral and floral motifs, which ends in a cusp with corolla rosette emerging from the line of the eaves. It also included ogee windows along the calle and the rose window in the façade, now suffocated by the excessively close neighbouring buildings.
The columns were replaced during a heavy restoration in 1804, when several windows were also opened up and others closed, and neo-classical decoration added. In the same operation, or perhaps another in the same century, the semi-circular apse enriched with a triple order of small loggias was demolished to make way for one that was internally semi-circular and externally semi-octagonal with simple ribbed windows.
In the latest restoration work the interior has been cleaned of its most recent superfetations, revealing in particular the splendid wooden, keel roof, similar to those in Santo Stefano and San Giacomo dall'Orio.

The Tiepolos

The area that would have been the narthex of the main entrance, which is now via the side door, comprises the Oratory of the Crucifix and houses the fourteen stations of the *Via Crucis* painted by Giandomenico Tiepolo between 1747 and 1749.
The name Tiepolo usually conjures up Giambattista's triumphal visions of light and colour, while the introverted character that marked his son, Giandomenico, is quite another thing. Even in his youth he had an embittered, gloomy temperament, drawn to grotesque representation and melancholy. But he was rarely able to work for himself, free of the constrictions of his father's workshop and his patrician commis-

32. Giandomenico Tiepolo
Episodes from the Via Crucis
1747-49

sions. On those few occasions, however, his brush revealed his true character.
One of these rare cases is precisely the *Via Crucis* in San Polo, entrusted to him when he was only a little more than twenty, possibly through the sponsorship of Alvise Cornaro. An unexpected spirit is revealed here: figures drawn with surprising realism; colours often shaded in melancholy tones of a pale, chalky white; acute drawing – often as biting as caricature.
It is a style of painting that seems quite ahead of its time, in a Venice that continued to be that of the interminable carnival – despite the city's imminent decline. The paternal style seems tied to those past triumphs achieved by the Republic, almost as if to exorcise the approaching end. But this is rather anticipated by the more honest works of the son: these do not retrace heroes, mythological gods and patrician families, but the daily life of people, and in a rural environment rather than suspended amongst the clouds.
San Polo also offers an opportunity to compare the style of father and son in the same building.

2. Jacopo Robusti called Tintoretto
Last Supper, 1568-69

11. Jacopo Negretti called Palma Giovane
St Peter sends St Mark to preach the Gospel in Aquileia, 1625

The eighteenth-century works that led to the creation of the oratory of the Crucifix with the *Via Crucis* also included the making of a new altar dedicated to St John of Nepomuk. This was made to a design by Giorgio Massari and bore the altarpiece by Giambattista showing the apparition of the Virgin to the saint. A precious relic of St John was donated to the church by King Augustus III of Saxony in 1740, and this allows the supposition of a direct commission from the King of Saxony to Giambattista, with whom he was certainly in contact through Francesco Algarotti.
But the altar was moved from its original position during the nineteenth-century rearrangements to a place where the light is not the same as that it was designed for, producing quite a different effect and making it impossible to admire the piece as it was originally conceived. The work of Giandomenico may be recognised in the architectural structure and the marginal figures. However, it is not of a particularly high level, with the exception of some elements, such as the palm and the creased book, painted with the easy touch, the rich, concise brush that typified the work of Giambattista.

Santa Maria Gloriosa dei Frari

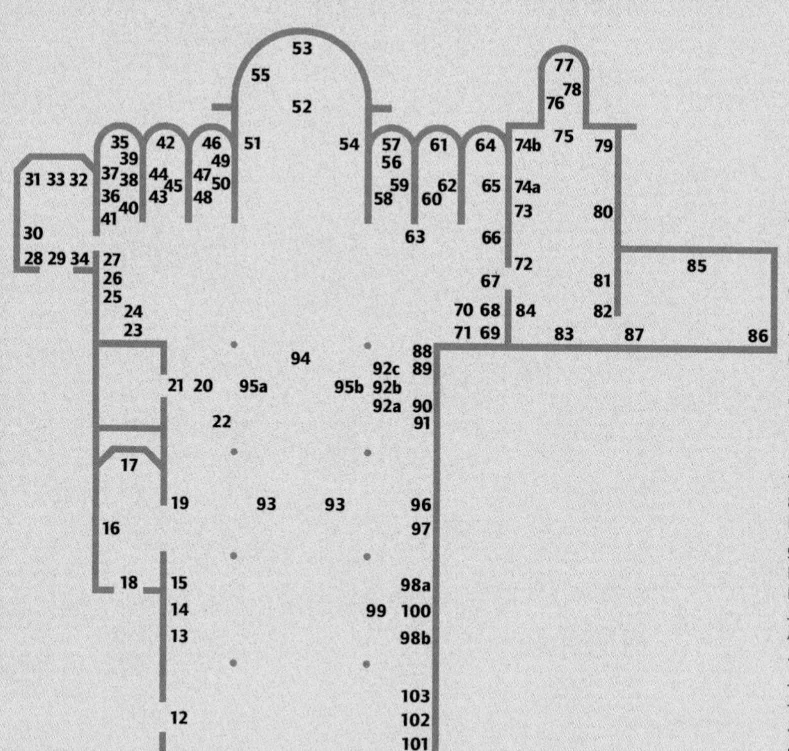

1. Anonymous, *Monument to Gerolamo Garzoni*, 1688

2. Lorenzo Bregno (attr.) *Monument to Alvise Pasqualigo*, 1528

3. Tullio Lombardo, *Monument to Pietro Bernardo*, post 1538

4. Flaminio Florian, *Eight Miracles of St Anthony*, XVII c.

5. Pietro Muttoni called Pietro della Vecchia, *St Anthony with a Model of the Saint's Church* XVII c.

6. Anonymous, *Monument to Senator Simonetto Dandolo* c. 1360

7. Angelo Venturini, *St John the Evangelist blesses the Disciples* XVIII c.

8. Baldassarre Longhena, Giusto Le Court, *Altar of the Crucifix*, 1672

9. Antonio Bosa, Giuseppe Fabris, Rinaldo Rinaldi, Bartolomeo Ferrari, Luigi Zandomeneghi, Jacopo de' Martini, *Monument to Antonio Canova*, 1822-27

10-11. Gerolamo Campagna, 1593
- *St Anthony*
- *Mansuetudine*

12. Baldassarre Longhena, Melchior Barthel, Bernardo Falcone da Lugano, *Monument to Doge Giovanni Pesaro*, 1660-69

13. Anonymous, *Burial urn of Giuseppe Volpi di Misurata*, XX c.

14. Tiziano Vecellio *Pesaro Altarpiece*, 1519-26

15. Lombardo workshop *Monument to Jacopo Pesaro*, 1524

16. St peter Chapel Circle of dalle Masegne *Monument to Bishop Pietro Miani*, 1464

17. St peter Chapel Anonymous, Tuscan, *Altar*, XV c.

18. St peter Chapel Anonymous, Veneto, *Crucifix*, XV c.

19. St peter Chapel Anonymous, *Monument to Gerolamo Venier*, XVII c.

20. St peter Chapel Anonymous, *Virgin and Child with Saints Francis and Anthony*, XIII c.

21. St peter Chapel Pietro Negri *The Franciscan Tree*, 1670

22. St peter Chapel Andrea Michieli called Vicentino *The Seven Works of Mercy*, XVII c.

23. St peter Chapel Lorenzo and Claudio Canozzi da Lendinara, *Dossal*, XV c.

24. St peter Chapel Pietro Lombardo (attr.) *Monument to Generosa Orsini and Maffeo Zen*, XV c.

25. St peter Chapel Andrea Michieli called Vicentino *Virgin and Christ in Glory with Saints*, XVII c.

26. St Peter Chapel
Andrea Celesti, *Massacre of the Innocents*, XVIII c.

27. St Peter Chapel
Andrea Michieli called Vicentino
The Bronze Serpent and the Crucifix, XVIII c.

28. Corner Chapel
Jacopo Tatti called Sansovino
St John the Baptist, 1554

29. Corner Chapel
Anonymous, *Baptismal font*, XIX c.

30. Corner Chapel
Anonymous, Tuscan, *Monument to Federico Corner*, XV c.

31. Corner Chapel
Stained glass: *The Virgin, St Sebastian, St Catherine of Alexandria, St Mark, St Gregory and St Lucy*, XV c.

32. Corner Chapel
Giovanni Beltrami
Stained glass, 1907

33. Corner Chapel
Bartolomeo Vivarini
St Mark Enthroned and Saints John the Baptist, Jerome, Peter and Nicholas, 1474

34. Corner Chapel
Jacopo Negretti called Palma Giovane
Descent into Limbo, c. 1600

35. Chapel of the Milanese
Alvise Vivarini, Marco Basaiti
St Ambrose Enthroned and Saints 1503

36-37. Chapel of the Milanese
Tiziano Vecellio called Tizianello
XVII c.
- *St Ambrose forbids the Emperor Entrance to the Temple*
- *St Charles Borromeo administers Communion to the Plague Victims*

38. Chapel of the Milanese
Giovanni Contarini, *St Ambrose expels the Aryans*, XVII c.

39. Chapel of the Milanese
Ludovico David, *St Charles Borromeo distributes Alms*, XVII c.

40. Chapel of the Milanese
Anonymous, *Bust of Claudio Monteverdi*, XIX c.

41. Chapel of the Milanese
Tomb of Claudio Monteverdi

42. St Michael Chapel
Veneto sculptor, *Altar of St Michael or of the Scuola dei Boccaleri*, XV c.

43. St Michael Chapel
Anonymous, *Monument to an unknown soldier*, XIV c.

44. St Michael Chapel
Giuseppe Angeli
Virgin and Saints, c. 1750

45. St Michael Chapel
Veneto sculptor, *Monument to Melchiorre Trevisan*, XVI c.

46-47. Chapel of the Franciscan Saints
Bernardino Licinio, XVI c.
- *Virgin and Child with Saints*
- *The Franciscan Protomartyrs*

48. Chapel of the Franciscan Saints
Andrea Michieli called Vicentino
St Francis obtains Approval from Pope Honorius III, XVII c.

49. Chapel of the Franciscan Saints
Jacopo Negretti called Palma Giovane, *St Francis obtains Approval from Pope Honorius III and Confirmation of the Order* 1598

50. Chapel of the Franciscan Saints
Anonymous, *Urn to Nicolò Lion* XIV c.

51. Chancel
Antonio Rizzo and assistants
Monument to Doge Niccolò Tron c. 1476

52. Chancel
Lorenzo Bregno (attr.)
Main altar, 1416-18

53. Chancel
Tiziano Vecellio
Assumption of the Virgin, 1518

54. Chancel
Niccolò di Giovanni Fiorentino
Monument to Doge Francesco Foscari († 1457)

55. Chancel
Anonymous, *Crucifix*, XIII c.

56. Chapel of St John the Baptist
Anonymous, Tuscan, *Altar*, XV c.

57. Chapel of St John the Baptist
Donato di Niccolò di Betto Bardi called Donatello
St John the Baptist, 1438

58. Chapel of St John the Baptist
Umberto Martina
St Francis Praying, 1945

59. Chapel of St John the Baptist
Ottavio Angaran, *Nativity*, XVII c.

60. Chapel of the Sacrament
Anonymous, *Monument to Arnoldo d'Este*, XIV c.

61. Chapel of the Sacrament
Vincenzo Cadorin, *Altar*, XIX c.

62. Chapel of the Sacrament
Anonymous, *Monument to Ambassador Duccio degli Alberti* XIV c.

63. Chapel of the Sacrament
Anonymous, *Bust of Christ*, XIII c.

64. Bernardo Chapel
Bartolomeo Vivarini
Virgin Enthroned and Child with Saints Andrew, Nicholas of Bari, Paul and Peter, 1482

65. Bernardo Chapel
Anonymous, *Urn of Gerolamo and Lorenzo Bernardo*, 1500

66. Anonymous, Tuscan
Monument to Paolo Savelli, XV c.

67. Giovan Battista Bregno
Monument to Benedetto Pesaro post 1503

68. Nanni di Bartolo called Rosso
Monument to Beato Pacifico, 1427

69. Giovanni di Francia (attr.)
Annunciation, XV c.

70. Pietro Lombardo, *Monument to Jacopo Marcello*, post 1488

71. Mantegnesque painter
Triumph of Jacopo Marcello post 1488

72. Sacristy
Francesco Pianta, *Clock*, XVII c.

73. Sacristy
Nicolò Frangipane
Deposition, 1593

74a-b. Sacristy
Bonifacio de' Pitati, XVI c.
- *The Queen of Sheba's Visit to Solomon*
- *Adoration of the Magi*

75. Sacristy
Jacopo Parisati di Montagnana
Annunciation, XV c.

76. Sacristy
Giambattista Pittoni
Hagar in the Desert, XVIII c.

77. Sacristy
Giovanni Bellini, *Virgin and Child with saints Nicholas, Peter, Benedict and Mark*, 1488

78. Sacristy
Circle of Giambattista Piazzetta
Susanna and the Elders, XVIII c.

79. Sacristy
Anonymous Veneto
Our Lady of Mercy, XV c.

80. Sacristy
Francesco da Santacroce or Polidoro de Renzi, *Mystic Marriage of St Catherine*, XVI c.

81. Sacristy
Francesco Penso called Cabianca, Andrea Brustolon
Altar of relics, 1711

82. Sacristy
Giambattista Salvi called Sassoferrato, *Madonna*, XVII c.

83. Sacristy
Paolo Veneziano, *Virgin and Child with St Francis and St Elizabeth accompanying the Doge and the Dogaressa*, 1339

84. Sacristy
Tullio Lombardo (attr.)
Marble sanctuary, XV c.

85. Chapter House
Anonymous, *Monument to Doge Andrea Dandolo*, post 1354

86. Chapter House
Old bell-tower mechanism

87. Chapter House
Anonymous, *Crucifixion*, XIX c.

88. Anonymous Veneto, *Tomb of Abbot Luigi della Torre*, 1549

89. Pietro Lombardo (attr.)
Monument to the philosopher Benedetto Brugnolo, XVI c.

90. Francesco Penso called Cabianca, *Monument to Bishop Francesco Bottari*, 1708

91. Matteo Carnelio, *Monument to Bishop Marco Zen*, 1641

92a-c. Andrea Michieli called Vicentino, XVII c.
- *Creation of the World*
- *The Bronze Serpent raised by Moses in the Desert*
- *Last Judgement and the Glory of Paradise*

93. Choir
Northern sculptors (from Strasbourg?) and Lombardo workshop
Marble structure of choir, XV c.

94. Choir
Marco Cozzi and Strasbourg sculptor
Wooden stalls, 1468

95a. Choir
Giovan Battista Piaggia
Organ, 1732

95b. Choir
Gaetano Callido, *Organ*, 1796

96. Jacopo Negretti called Palma Giovane, *Martyrdom of St Catherine*, 1590-95

97. Workshop of Antonio Lombardo, *Monument to Captain Jacopo Barbaro*, 1511

98a-b-99. Alessandro Vittoria 1564
- *St Peter*
- *St Andrew*
- *St Jerome*

100. Giuseppe Nogari
St Joseph of Copertino in Glory XVIII c.

101. Anonymous, *Monument to the Prince of Modena Almerico d'Este commander of the auxiliary troops in the war of Candia* († 1666)

102-103. Giuseppe Porta called Salviati, c. 1550-60
- *Presentation of Jesus at the Temple*
- *Prophets*

104. Luigi and Pietro Zandomeneghi, *Monument to Titian*, 1838-52

105. Baldassarre Longhena, Giuseppe Sardi
Altar of St Anthony, XVII c.

106. Giacomo di Caterino
St Anthony, 1450

107. Bernardo Falcone da Lugano, *Christ Arisen*, XVII c.

108. Francesco Rosa
St Anthony of Padua raises his Father, 1670

Origins

The Grey Friars of the Order of St Francis came to Venice in about 1222, living according to the Order on charity and by menial work. They obtained permission from the government to settle in a small, old, abandoned Benedictine abbey dedicated to the Virgin and situated in the same area as the current complex. In about 1236 Doge Jacopo Tiepolo gave the friars a large tract of land alongside, the 'lago Badoer', where, with donations from the government and the public, they began transforming and extending the conventual building. Then, in 1250, work began on a new church. This was consecrated in 1280, and was probably oriented in the opposite direction to that of the present church.

The importance of the Franciscan Order within the community grew significantly over the years on both a political and devotional level, so much so that by 1330 there was already talk of a new building. Construction on this got under way in 1340, starting with the apsidal chapel and the transept, completed in 1361. Work on the mighty bell tower – one of the highest in the city – also began in that year. This was built to a design by Jacopo Celega, who probably also supervised construction of the church; the bell tower was finished by his son, Pietro Paolo, in 1396. The decision to begin work with the apses and rotate the orientation of the church was common practice as it allowed services to continue in the old building until the new one was functional. Alteration of the longitudinal axis oriented to the Rialto-San Marco's line, and construction of the bridge in front of the façade, in 1428, also put the new temple in direct communication with the city centre. Its growing importance seems confirmed by the numerous donations made by powerful Venetian families and others, and by the requests from many art schools and corporations to place their altars in the church. This quickly made the Frari into one of the most important and vibrant monastic centres in the city. Despite this, there were several delays in construction work and the building was not completed until the 1430s or 40s. Other structures were erected in the course of that same century resulting in a very grandiose complex, made up of the external Corner, Bernardo and Pesaro chapels – the latter now the sacristy– chapter house, refectory, three cloisters, gardens and convent. With suppression and state appropriation in 1810, the church and library were badly damaged, while the convent was turned into a State Archive in 1814 after a period as a barracks. The parish was eventually reinstituted and entrusted to the conventual Grey Friars.

Exterior

The church is 102 metres in length and rises powerfully in terracotta, once faced with imitation brick marbling – of which a few remnants can still be seen. It faces onto a fairly wide *campo* lapped by the rio dei Frari,

94. Marco Cozzi and Strasbourg sculptor
Wooden stalls, 1468

53. Tiziano Vecellio
Assumption of the Virgin, 1518

but the real, much larger *campo*, is faced by the left side of the building, while the apsidal side runs along salizzada di San Rocco.
All the external decoration is typical Gothic, with high windows, cornices of small hanging arches, lesenes, rose windows and monumental doorways sculpted from Istrian and red Verona stone with splayed ogee arches and statues or pinnacles. The façade follows the usual three divisions mirroring the internal nave and side aisle layout, with a poly-lobed coping surmounting the cornices, completed by three cuspidal niches – of which there were originally five.
The size of the church is particularly striking, such that it can be noticed even behind the curtain of other buildings, like something apart from the building fabric which almost vibrates in the air.

Interior

The interior does not disappoint: it is just as fascinating and monumental as the outside – and it could also be regarded as a museum by the quantity and quality of works it contains. Although breached by the large main chapel, the structure is basically that of an Egyptian cross, or tau, one of the recurring symbols of St Francis and his churches. The last letter of the Hebrew language, it is a sign of salvation, associated with the shape of Christ's cross and that of the Grey Friar's frock. It reappears in the layout of the Franciscan churches of Santa Croce in Florence, the Upper basilica in Assisi and San Francesco della Vigna in Venice. The twelve powerful round pillars represent the apostles, pillars of the Church. These provide the base for the ogee ribbed cross vaults that cover the whole of the building, in some places broad, in others narrow. The main structure includes side altars along the aisles and seven chapels along the transept. Other external structures are adjoined to this form: the bell tower, the St Peter and Corner chapels, the sacristy and the conventual complex.

The choir

The last broad bay of the nave is taken up a monks' choir. There were once various examples of these in Venice, demolished after the Council of Trent and later reassembled in different ways, but this example can still be admired in all its original splendour.
The effect of the choir is quite exceptional. Although it obstructs the view to the base of the apse, it is actually a scenographic wing whose marble doorway frames the spiritual, symbolic and figurative centre of the entire church: Titian's *Assumption of the Virgin* on the main altar. It conspires to concentrate attention on the painting which shines down in all

53. Tiziano Vecellio
Assumption of the Virgin, 1518
detail

its splendour. Standing in the choir is equally interesting; it is almost a building within a building. The choir is an imposing and not easily attributed Renaissance structure or, perhaps better, from that typically Venetian Transitional period. Inside, the wooden choir comprises three tiers of high dossals with intarsia work and carving, ending in a painted, gilt shell surmounted by an acute pinnacle at whose peak is the golden figure of an angel. Separated in *Zellenstip*, or into clearly divided cellular modules, the stalls repeat forms commonly found in Cistercian churches. The carvings on the upper part of the back section are by different hands: they represent Franciscan Saints, other less distinguishable Saints, the Virgin and Child, Christ benedictory and the Archangel Michael. Some have extremely fine intarsia work while others seem carved in a more rough and approximate manner. The marble screen that closes the choir off from outside is the work of several hands and difficult to place. A Lombardesque style can be identified in some panels with the Doctors of the Church, and Angels bearing the monogram of Saint Bernard at the upper sides and above the side doors that lead to the organs. There are then fourteen prophets at the sides of the large entrance arch and four at the sides of the choir. It is possible that in this case, too, a not easily identified northern European workshop was involved. The carvings of eight Apostles are attributed to Vittore Camelio while the Saints Anthony and Francis, the Virgin and Saint John beside the Crucifix are attributed to Andrea Verrocchio.

Titian and the church of the Frari

The special relationship between the most famous Venetian painter of the sixteenth century and the Frari is demonstrated by the two important works still kept here, but especially by his tomb. The *Assumption of the Virgin* was commissioned in 1516 and displayed for the first time in 1518. The theology of the Assumption had long been meditated and elaborated from a doctrinal point of view and was an intense part of the devotional life of the Church. Its feast had been celebrated in the East since the fifth century and in the West a little later under the Byzantine name of *Koimesis* (*Dormitio*), changed after a century into *Assumptio*. For the Frari the feast was fixed on the 15 August right from the laying of the first stone of the church, dedicated to Santa Maria Gloriosa dei Frari, in 1250. The dogma was proclaimed by Pius XIII in 1950. This prerogative of Mary, to ascend into Heaven in body, derives from her freedom of sin, from the fullness of Grace and from her divine maternity. The glory of Mary anticipates the future glory of the whole of humanity.
The story of the Virgin is condensed in Titian's radiant altarpiece. The oldest representation of the Assumption is a Western design from the seventh century, with Mary being transported to heaven by angels. This was followed by the Eastern *Koimesis* or *Dormitio*, widely circulated in the West after 1000 and represented in a variety of ways. In the Renaissance there was a return to the iconography of the Assumption, which Titian then updated and enlivened, with the heavenly flight of Mary from earth to heaven while the apostles, witnesses to the event, raise

their arms and the Holy Father stoops down to welcome her among the angels. A small angel can also be seen near the Holy Father, holding a crown, suggesting the subsequent Coronation of the Virgin. The painting was so innovative in comparison with traditional religious painting, particularly with the iconography of the Assumption, and in the agitated arrangement of the huge figures and bright polychromy, that it was received with some disapproval. Indeed, only a purchase offer from the Austrian ambassador convinced the friars not to turn it down. The holy episode is played out in three superimposed bands: the apostles and the earth, the Virgin surrounded by cherubs indicating the moment of Mary's passage from humanity to divinity, and the Holy Father amongst the clouds. The monumentality of the figures is accentuated by the vivid colours, the bright tones, the reds and greens of the apostles' cloaks and the deep red of the Virgin's dress. In the upper part of the composition, in the unreal light of an incandescent sunset, where the golden and ethereal faces of the cherubs seem transparent, the figure of the Holy Father, emerging from the thick covering of light, concludes and exalts the sacred event; 'the greatness and awesomeness of Michelangelo, the gracefulness and beauty of Raphael' (C. Dolce, 1548), are concentrated like this for the first time in the masterpiece of a young Venetian painter. In the thirteenth century, Saint Bonaventura said, 'What great splendour there will be, when the eternal sun illuminates the spirits ascended into glory'. And this glory is the light that is experienced in God. The light finally revealed. This is why Mary is said to be glorious. The Marian themes of the Immaculate Conception and the Assumption are illustrated in several masterpieces in the church, not only because these were traditionally dear to the Franciscan Order, but also because in the fifteenth century the Immaculate Conception had become a matter of theological contention, lively debated between Dominicans and Franciscans. The former emphasised the presence of evil in the story, while the latter presented oppressed and tormented humanity with an example modelled on man made victorious over evil by the Grace of God. The altar conceded to the Pesaro family in 1518 – the most generous benefactors to the Frari – had previously been dedicated to the Immaculate Conception in 1361. The altarpiece, commissioned by Jacopo Pesaro in 1519, illustrated a Marian theme as much as the glories of the family and the mediating presence of the Order. The white veil covering the heads of the Virgin and Child alludes to the shroud of pain and death that was to enfold both; while the two angels showing a dark and impending cross from the clouds refer more explicitly to the same theme. The political function is represented by the large group of Pesaro family members kneeling in the foreground and, in particular, by Jacopo, on the left. Victor over the Turks in the battle of Santa Maura and later Bishop of Pafos, he was therefore defender and guarantor of faith. The red flag in the background with two coats of arms, that of Pope Alexander VI and the Pesaro family, the soldier and the Turk with turban all refer to the abovementioned military glory. A boy on the right looks out towards the audience, almost drawing them into the picture. The intense exchange of looks between the va-

14. Tiziano Vecellio
Pesaro Altarpiece
1519-26

rious figures develops the motive behind the intercession. Mary looks at the apostle Peter who turns to the kneeling Jacopo; on the other side the Child and Francis look at one another. Titian did not finish the altarpiece until 1526, due probably to some rethinking. In the definitive version the bold perspective is accentuated by two mighty columns rising endlessly to create an illusory architecture that denies the physical limits of the altarpiece, projecting the scene into open space from which a white light spreads, lighting up the silky white of the Virgin's veil, the clothes of the young Pesaro and the Turk's turban, and warming on the pinks, yellows and browns. Titian died during the terrible plague of 1576 which devastated Venice and contrary to the strict sanitary laws applied in these cases, the painter's body was taken to the church of the Frari and buried in the nave, according to his will, surrounded by his masterpieces. In the mid-eighteenth century, Emperor Ferdinand I of Austria commissioned a funeral monument to properly honour the artist. The trium-

77. Giovanni Bellini
Virgin and Child with Saints Nicholas, Peter, Benedict and Mark, 1488

phal arch structure is surmounted by the lion of St Mark, with the artist in the centre between various figures and a sculpted copy of his Assumption of the Virgin behind, in what seems a confused work, typical of the composite style of much mid-eighteenth century art.

Giovanni Bellini

Another extraordinary work, by Bellini, hangs in the sacristy – originally built as the Pesaro Chapel. Commissioned by the Pesaro family, this time by Benedetto in 1478, it was completed by the artist in his maturity in 1488. The big main altarpiece is composed of three panels enclosed in an impressive gilt frame which creates the illusion of an entrance into a large room, almost an apsidal chapel, open at the sides onto two strips of landscape just glimpsed between the pillars of the frame and the painted ones. While these strips filter a clear, crystalline light, the gold of the mosaic decorated vault and the wall behind the Virgin reflect a warm light onto her figure – in a pyramid structure on high throne that is still quite traditional – which then dissolves in the depth of the apse, echoing the Lombardesque. The carved decoration of the frame is also Lombardesque: architecture that recalls buildings of that period, such as Santa Maria dei Miracoli, in the extraordinary harmony of its forms and relationships. The figures in the narrow space at the sides of the apse are solemnly impressive, amongst whom St Benedict is strangely turned towards the observer, almost as if to invite his participation in the Adoration of the Virgin.

The Vivarini

The numerous masterpieces in the Frari, include several paintings by the Vivarini. The altar in the Corner chapel bears an impressive wooden altarpiece carved and gilded in traditional late Gothic style, though the two figures of the Annunciation at the sides of the frame in the central section betray elements of a new language, in the self-assured spatiality of the forms and in the typology of the archaising structure. It frames the tryptych by Bartolomeo depicting *St Mark Enthroned and Saints John the Baptist, Jerome, Peter and Nicholas,* painted in 1474. St Mark's marble throne, in Lombardesque manner, clashes with the frame of the altarpiece: the two parts of the work are separated by a completely different spatiality. The wooden altarpiece becomes a window beyond which the scene of the holy representation unfolds around the figure of Mark, in a virtually single space, where the wings of the angels at the Saint's feet and the steps beneath the throne seem to continue under the balusters of the frame. Unlike Giovanni Bellini, Vivarini rejects the altarpiece as part of a language that can no longer be reconciled with his own. The bright colours, in variations of changing orange-reds in the parts struck by light, match the gold of the structure, taking up the warm, bright signs and thereby using colour to achieve the union that a different interpretation of space had made impossible. Bartolomeo painted his last polyptych in 1482 for the altar

of the Bernardo Chapel, with the *Virgin Enthroned and Child with Saints Andrew, Nicholas of Bari, Paul and Peter.* After eight years Vivarini's manner had completely changed: all trace of those late Gothic reminders in the previous altarpiece had by now been lost in the composed classicism of the forms. The architecture of the frame, which opens up like a gallery before the figures, remains completely independent of the painting, where a continuous staircase, on which saints and throne rest, creates the new spatial autonomy of the holy scene. And the canvas behind the Virgin, blocking off sight of the background, almost forms a niche by optical effect, allowing an apsidal space to be reconstructed around the Virgin by the placement of the saints' bodies at the sides. The clear light of an undefined background, the tones of colour, veering through different shades of red, from the lacquered red of the Virgin's dress to the orange tones of the saints', though mixed with greens and yellow in St Paul's cloak, highlight the extraordinary sense of balance the artist had by now completely attained – perhaps also taking a cue from Giovanni Bellini.
Alvise Vivarini, Bartolomeo's nephew, also painted for the Frari, producing the altarpiece in the Chapel of the Milanesi in 1503, left unfinished and completed by Marco Basaiti. The latter added subtones to Alvise's dense, glazed paint with a lighter, more opaque brush. The architecture of the carved, gilt frame seems to complete the painting, constituting the threshold over which the saint presents himself for the devotion of the faithful.

Florentine art in the Frari

Amongst the large number of sculptures enriching the Frari, two works in particular stand out. Small in size but of enormous value, both are of St John the Baptist, and both by celebrated Florentine artists. The first is on the altar of the Chapel of St John the Baptist, and was sculpted by Donatello in 1438, at the time working on the Florence cathedral. He was almost certainly chosen by the Florentine community in Venice with the intention of affirming the superiority – especially artistic – of their city, one of the main centres of the Renaissance in the first half of the century. Florentine culture was at that time well ahead of the Venetian, still lingering in late Gothic forms. The study of naturalistic phenomena Donatello had pursued since his earliest works emerges in the lean figure of the saint, in the tense face and in the bony hands. The saint is shown in the act of speaking, though signs of unease are clearly evident in his sinewy body, disarrayed hair and dissimilar eyes, elements that are nevertheless part of the Baptist's iconographic range.
The other John the Baptist, by Jacopo Sansovino, was originally in the side aisle but moved to the Corner Chapel at the beginning of the twentieth century. Sculpted around 1554, it was placed on the basin of the baptismal font donated by the Giustiniani family in 1826. The right arm was probably reconstructed on that occasion, in a different marble and out of anatomical proportion with the left, and was definitively removed in a recent restoration.

33. Bartolomeo Vivarini
St Mark Enthroned and Saints John the Baptist, Jerome, Peter and Nicholas, 1474

The Frari as pantheon

The number and value of funerary monuments in the dei Frari Basilica make it a genuine pantheon: doges, military leaders and artists have for five centuries requested burial here. Indeed, if viewed in their entirety, they offer a very interesting panorama of the development of this specific branch of art and sculpture; the oldest in the history of man and possibly the richest in spiritual, emotional and spiritual meanings.

Two of the oldest and most important of these face one another in the chancel. One to Doge Francesco Foscari, who died in 1457, attributed to Niccolò di Giovanni Fiorentino on the right wall, and the other to Doge Niccolò Tron, by Antonio Rizzo and assistants from around 1476, on the left.

The architectural structure of the first still seems linked to elements of a late flamboyant Gothic, quite openly declared by the large curtain overhanging the body of the deceased and held open by two shield-bearing pageboys to create a kind of niche, and the rigid structure of the sarcophagus with three panels showing figures of the theological virtues supported on corbels. This internal part, richer in Gothic references, is framed by a square structure resting on two tall columns whose form and type of decoration indicate the artist's interest in the Tuscan Renaissance funeral style, though this once again disappears in the characteristic fiery Gothic of the pediment. The rich painted and gilt decoration accentuates the preciousness of the material in the picturesque nature of the monument, typical of late Gothic culture.

The Tron monument, on the other hand, reveals Antonio Rizzo's now total command of Renaissance language in its grandiose structure and equilibrium. It is clearly a significant move forward in the history of funeral monuments: the deceased is no longer shown simply lying on the

83. Paolo Veneziano
Virgin and Child with St Francis and St Elizabeth accompanying the Doge and the Dogaressa, 1339

sarcophagus, but in both life and death. Once deceased and once on foot in his ducal vestments with lively, concentrated look. Rizzo's work is arranged into four overlapping areas. The lower band shows the doge with Faith and Charity in three arches; the second bears the commemorative inscription and his coats of arms; in the third he rests on the sarcophagus adorned with antique medallions and figures alluding to the virtues of man: Prudence, Abundance and Strength. Other Virtues are aligned along the fourth band, while the risen Christ and the Annunciation in the lunette allude to the redemption and resurrection of the dead. Two other grandiose funeral monuments are of note: one already mentioned to Titian, and the other to Antonio Canova. The latter was constructed by his students and completed in 1827 on the model of one made by Canova for Maria Christina of Austria. The pyramid structure with various figures in mourning recalls Canova models from a period of pure Venetian neo-classicism. A striking effect is achieved by the door left half-open towards the inside where the artist's heart is preserved; his body is buried in Possagno.

San Giacomo dall'Orio

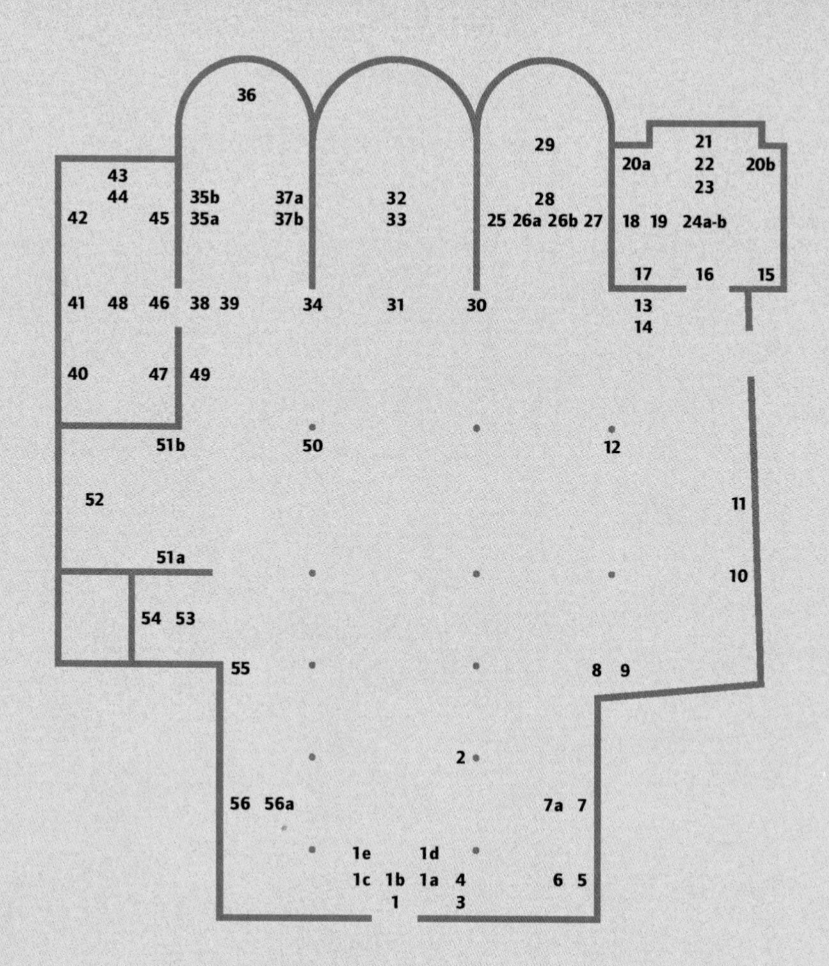

1. Gaetano Callido
Organ, 1776

1a-e. Andrea Meldolla
called Schiavone, XVI c.
- *The Calling of St James*
- *The Preaching of St James*
- *The Martyrdom of St James*
- *Elderly King David*
- *King David*

2. Anonymous
Four-lobed stoup, XIII c.

3. Giuseppe Camerata
The Virgin appears to St Jerome Emiliani, XVIII c.

4. Gaetano Zompini
Miracle of the Virgin, XVIII c.

5. Jacopo Negretti
called Palma Giovane (attr.)
Christ supported by an Angel, c. 1600

6. Anonymous
Last Supper, XVI c.

7. Anonymous
Madonna, XV c.

7a. Anonymous
Madonna of the Rosary
altar frontal, XVI c.

8. Anonymous, *Virgin Praying*
XIII c.

9. Jacopo Negretti
called Palma Giovane
Miracles of the Loaves and Fishes, c. 1614

10. Anonymous
Urn of Clara Priuli, XVI c.

11. Giambattista Pittoni
Virgin and Child in Glory with Saints, 1764

12. *Column in antique green marble with Ionic capital*, VI c.

13. Anonymous
Supper at Emmaus, XV c.

14. Anonymous, *Adoration of the Sheperds*, XVI c.

15. New sacristy
Francesco Zugno
Presentation of Jesus at the Temple, c. 1771

16. New sacristy
Giambattista Cromer
Virgin with Saints Anne, Joachim, Anthony of Padua, Joseph and Francis Sales
1743

17. New sacristy
Francesco Bassano
Virgin with Saints John the Baptist and Nicholas of Bari, XVI c.

18. New sacristy
Tiziano Vecellio
called Tizianello (attr.)
Agony in the Garden, XVI c.

19. New sacristy
Melchiorre Colonna
The Washing of the Feet
XVIII c.

20a-b. New sacristy
Anonymous, XVIII c.
- *St Anthony*
- *St Eustace*

21. New sacristy
Francesco Bassano
and assistants
Preaching of St John the Baptist, c. 1570

22. New sacristy
Freize in gilt and blue wood
fragment of church decoration

23. New sacristy
Workshop of Bonifacio de' Pitati
Marriage at Cana, XVI c.

24a-b. Ceiling of the New sacristy
Paolo Caliari
called Veronese (attr.), 1577
- *Faith and the Holy Spirit*
- *Doctors of the Church*

25. Chapel of the Holy Sacrament
Giulio del Moro
Ecce Homo, XVI c.

26a-b. Chapel of the Holy Sacrament
Jacopo Negretti called
Palma Giovane, c. 1604
- *Via Crucis*
- *Burial of Christ*

27. Chapel of the Holy Sacrament
Tiziano Vecellio
called Tizianello
Flagellation, XVI c.

28. Ceiling of the Chapel of the Holy Sacrament
Alessandro Varotari
called Padovanino
The Four Evangelists, XVII c.

29. Dome frescoes of the Chapel of the Holy Sacrament
Jacopo Guarana, *Glory of the Holy Sacrament with Musician Angels*, 1753

30. Dome frescoes of the Chapel of the Holy Sacrament
Bortolo Cabianca
St James, 1671

31. Chancel
Paolo Veneziano (attr.)
Crucifix, c. 1350

32. Chancel
Lorenzo Lotto, *Virgin and Child with Saints*, 1546

33. Chancel
Anonymous, *Martyrdom of St James the Apostle*
altar frontal, 1704

34. Anonymous, *Virgin Annunciata*, XIV c.

35a-b. Left Chapel
Andrea Meldolla
called Schiavone, c. 1532
- *St John the Evangelist*
- *St James*

36. Left Chapel
Lorenzo Gramiccia
Addolorata, 1770

37a-b. Left Chapel
Gualtiero Padovano, XVI c.
- *Daniel*
- *David*

38. Anonymous
Angel, XIII c.

39. Anonymous
Virgin and Child, XIII c.

40-47. Old sacristy
Jacopo Negretti called
Palma Giovane, 1580-81
- *Elijah fed by the Angel*
- *The Fall of Manna*
- *The Bronze Serpent*
- *Virgin with Saints James, Silvester and Mark, and the Vicar Da Ponte*
- *Crucifix with the Virgin and St John*
- *Parting of the Red Sea*
- *Christ laid in the Sepulchre*
- *Paschal Lamb*

48. Ceiling of the Old sacristy
Jacopo Negretti called
Palma Giovane, 1580-81
The Blessed and the Four Evangelists

49. Giovanni Buonconsiglio
Saints Sebastian, Roch and Laurence, 1498-1500

50. Anonymous
Pulpit, XVI c.

51a-b. Chapel of St Laurence Martyr
Jacopo Negretti called
Palma Giovane, 1581-82
- *Martyrdom of St Laurence*
- *Distributing the Holy Riches to the Poor*

52. Chapel of St Laurence Martyr
Paolo Caliari
called Veronese
Saints Laurence, Jerome and Prosper, c. 1581

53. Baptistry
Anonymous, *Basin in red Verona marble*, XVI c.

54. Baptistry
Veneto School
Baptism of Christ, XVI c.

55. Antonio Palma
Miracle of St James raising the Cook, XVI c.

56. Anonymous
Marble Crucifix, XVII c.

56a. Anonymous, *The Virgin and the Three Maries*
altar frontal, XVII c.

The building

The church of San Giacomo is one of the oldest and most interesting in Venice, standing almost isolated in one of the few *campi* of a reasonable size in the city. Its façade is turned towards a small *campo* lapped by the rio di San Giacomo, while the other three sides face onto the surrounding campo di San Giacomo.
The exterior is fairly austere on all four sides, but the interior is a real revelation, with quite a unique atmosphere.

Origins

The original foundation of the building seems to date from the ninth-tenth century, though the first official document relating to it is dated 1089. In any case, in 1225 the patrician Badoer and Da Mula families financed its total reconstruction on a basilica layout with nave and aisles and particular elements such as the green marble column with Ionic capital, brought back from Byzantium as a trophy from the fourth crusade.
Subsequent restorations made fairly dramatic changes to the planimetric and volumetric arrangement.
The most significant transformation took place at the end of the fourteenth century and the first half of the fifteenth: a transept with nave and aisles was added, along with an apse, divided externally by lesenes and crowned with a band of small hanging arches; an upper one of small pillars being added later. Inside, columns, capitals and arches were replaced with others in clearly Gothic style but, most importantly, the wooden, three-lobed keel roof was built in the same style as those of the same period on Santo Stefano and San Polo.
During the Renaissance, sculpted and gilded wooden cornices were added along the nave and apse, and the chancel enriched with elegant marble reliefs. A general restoration of the apses was also made, through to construction of the Chapel of the Holy Sacrament in 1549.
Despite these alterations, the interior of the church maintains its unity with an overall archaic feel.

43. Jacopo Negretti called Palma Giovane
Virgin with Saints James, Silvester and Mark, and the Vicar Da Ponte, 1580-81

48. Jacopo Negretti called Palma Giovane
The Blessed and the Four Evangelists, 1580-81

Palma Giovane: the Old sacristy

The cycle commissioned from Palma Giovane by the vicar Giovanni Maria Da Ponte for the sacristy of his church, completed in 1581, aroused considerable interest not only in the context of the artist's development, but also in relation to the new directions of the post-Tridentine Church. It is perhaps the first pictorial cycle in Venice to portray the Eucharist in the dual sense defined by the Council of Trent, as

sacrifice and sacrament, arranging these according to a preordained theological scheme. The Tridentine Church had centralised the Eucharist as the sacrament *par excellence*, and its visualisation had to be not only triumphalistic, but also more closely connected to the holy sources. In short, it was necessary to trace a grand epic, in an effort to combat ignorance and doubt, right through from the Old Testament, with episodes symbolically foretelling the Eucharistic mystery, to the Gospel, with the consummation of the sacrifice on the Cross. With the traditional iconography of the Last Supper now superseded, artists began to portray those who had experienced and recounted it: the evangelists. The strict theme, though in varying examples, found support in the language of Palma, here in his first complex religious commission after his return from Rome. His is primarily a clearer, higher level of expression than that which was to be defined Venetian late Mannerism.
The works range from the Bassanesque atmosphere of the nocturnal candle-lit scene of the *Paschal Lamb*, alluding to the altar table and the sacrifice made there each time mass is celebrated, to an analysis of the various episodes in the *Parting of the Red Sea*. The Eucharistic significance can here be read in relation to Christ, who offers freedom from moral slavery with his sacrifice, and in the symbolic blood of Christ-Red Sea (there is probably also a political inference here, as a record of the recent victory of Lepanto in which Venice had beaten the Turk, enemy of the faith). The artist's Roman Mannerist schooling led him to move the most important figures to the background in the big canvas, leaving the nudes and decorative figures in the foreground and allowing displays of formal cognition, such as in *The Fall of Manna*, prelude to the institution of the Sacrament powerfully expressed by Christ himself. The *Four Evangelists* in the middle of the ceiling are the hub of the entire cycle, because the Eucharist is no longer depicted allusively through episodes from the Old Testament, but is now represented in its essence of glory and real presence, in a scene crammed with Tridentine theological meanings.
The artist's independence from various fixed models is evident in this cycle, as it is in the nearby Malipiero Chapel, where Palma painted the two canvases *Distributing the Holy Riches to the Poor* and the *Martyrdom of St Laurence* soon after. This is a delicate moment of transfer after the impact of the mysterious world of the late Titian – and the fragment of live coal under the gridiron takes on the form of a homage to the altarpiece on the same subject in the church of the Jesuits. But the haunted tension of the tragedy of the individual is here transposed into choral form, enlivened by elements taken from daily life, where episodes marked by a descriptive naturalism must still be read in a Tridentine context, under the influence of the Theatine spiritual current presenting the holy martyr as the model of a poor Catholic Church that distributed even its liturgical wealth to the needy.
It is already possible to anticipate a constant in Jacopo's approach to the ecclesiastical or more generically devotional themes that were to play a major part in his overall production in these first works. Never as in

32. Lorenzo Lotto
Virgin and Child with Saints, 1546

this period was there such competition between the churches, even by solicitation with pastoral visits, to decorate altars with pieces extolling the dogma of the Catholic Church, and between the Brotherhoods and Schools, both religious and lay, to decorate their chapels with new pictorial cycles, particularly those of the Holy Sacrament. It was largely a spontaneous movement, at least in Venice, seemingly indicative of the new place taken up by the individual within society, and therefore also of community life. Palma seems to have belonged to that category of artist compliant with the teachings of the Church, in perfect harmony with the religious thinking of his time. So much so that his paintings are often models of communication and narration, suggesting the existence of a substantial accord between the artist and the faithful.

32. Lorenzo Lotto
Virgin and Child with Saints, 1546
details

Palma Giovane:
chapel of the Holy Sacrament

The *Via Crucis* and the *Burial of Christ* are two splendid works, amongst Palma's greatest achievements in his long working life. The compositional structure extended to meet the requirements of the space obliged Jacopo to renew his iconography, to lay down a horizontal rhythm linked by a certain Tintoretto inspired – though quite autonomous – style in the contained severity of the colour, showing certain Tintoretto-like solutions in the faces. But there is no doubt that the greatest inspiration was the art of Titian. In the *Burial*, the tract of landscape on the left with the light of fiery sunset is clearly of Titianesque inspiration, but it is assimilated and recreated to succeed as something quite independent. The last exalted moment of a painter born with Giorgione seems to live here, and destined also to end here. These canvases must certainly be numbered amongst the masterpieces of Venetian painting at the end of the century.

The chancel works

In addition to a splendid Crucifix hanging from the intrados, attributed to Paolo Veneziano, the chancel houses a large altar piece by Lorenzo Lotto, one of the few pieces in Venice by this most restless of Italian Renaissance artists. Although a native of Venice, Lotto worked mainly elsewhere, in Lombardy and the Marches.

It is a version of a well-known composition: the Virgin and Child enthroned on a background of rich green drapery being crowned by two angels. In the left foreground, St James holds a stick, the classical sign of the pilgrim, with his knapsack next to him, while St Andrew on the right leans on the cross of martyrdom. Beside them and further back are two medical saints, Cosma and Damian, one of whom is holding a spatula and the other a pharmaceutical jar. The presence of these is due to the dedication of the altar, but there may also have been a personal meaning for Lotto. He was recovering from an illness between August and December 1546 when working on the altar piece. Signs of this may perhaps also be found in the painting itself, with its simplification and poverty of inspiration, favouring the mystical moment typical of popular piety. The warm, luminous colouring, even if in subdued tones, has been recently brought back to light thanks to a masterful restoration.

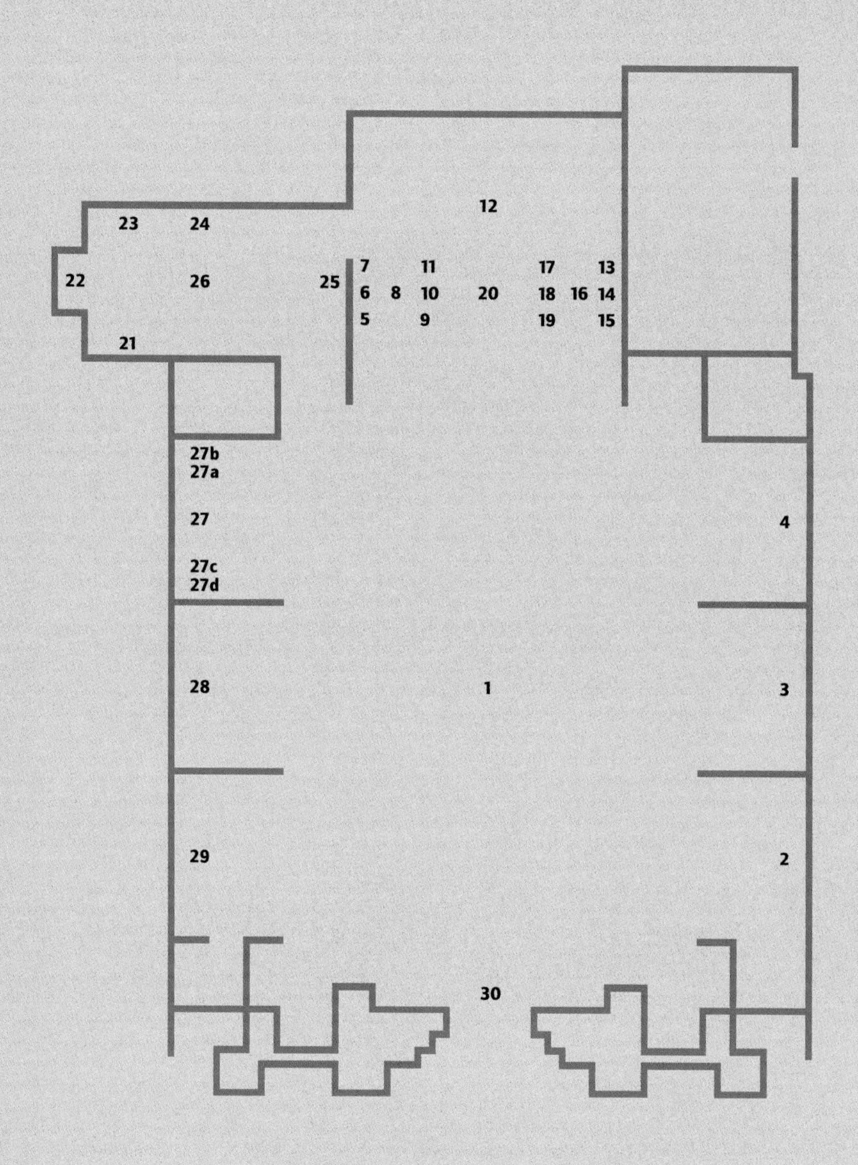
12
23
24
7
11
17
13
22
26
25
6
8
10
20
18
16
14
5
9
19
15
21
27b
27a
27
4
27c
27d
28
1
3
29
2
30

1. Anonymous, *Gravestone of the Mocenigo family*, XVIII c.

2. Nicolò Bambini
Virgin and Saints Laurence Giustiniani, Francis of Assisi and Anthony of Padua, c. 1710

3. Giuseppe Camerata
St Eustace, post 1710

4. Antonio Balestra
St Oswald, c. 1710

5. Chancel
Silvestro Manaigo
St Matthew, c. 1720

6. Chancel
Giambattista Mariotti
St Simon, c. 1725

7. Chancel
Angelo Trevisani
St Jude Thaddaeus, c. 1721

8. Chancel
Giuseppe Angeli, *Sacrifice of Melchisedech*, post 1770

9. Chancel
Giambattista Tiepolo
Martyrdom of St Bartholomew
1722

10. Chancel
Sebastiano Ricci
Liberation of St Peter, 1717-24

11. Chancel
Antonio Balestra
St John the Evangelist Martyred, c. 1725

12. Chancel
Giuseppe Torretto
Christ removed from the Cross and Angels, altar frontal
XVIII c.

13. Chancel
Pietro Uberti, *St Philip struck by a Soldier*, 1722-23

14. Chancel
Nicolò Bambini
St James the Less, 1722-23

15. Chancel
Giambattista Pittoni
Martyrdom of St Thomas
1722-23

16. Chancel
Giuseppe Angeli
The Fall of Manna, 1722-23

17. Chancel
Giambattista Piazzetta
St James the Great, 1717

18. Chancel
Gregorio Lazzarini, *St Paul ascends into Heaven*, 1722-23

19. Chancel
Giovanni Antonio Pellegrini
Crucifixion of St Andrew
1722-23

20. Ceiling of the Chancel
Bartolomeo Litterini
The Virtues and Two Brothers of the Scuola del Santissimo, 1708

21. Sacristy
School of Giambattista Tiepolo
St Eustace and the Emperor
post 1753

22. Sacristy
Maffeo Verona
Crucifixion, XVII c.

23. Sacristy
Giambattista Pittoni
The Emperor orders Sacrifice to the Idols, 1722

24. Sacristy
Bartolomeo Litterini
St Eustace in Prison, XVIII c.

25. Sacristy
Pietro Muttoni
called Pietro della Vecchia
Dead Christ, XVII c.

26. Ceiling of the Sacristy
Anonymous, German
Resurrection, 1686

27. Foscarini Chapel
Giuseppe Torretto
Crucifix, c. 1700

27a. Foscarini Chapel
Antonio Tarsia, *Bust of Antonio Foscarini*, XVIII c.

27b. Foscarini Chapel
Giuseppe Torretto, *Bust of Sebastiano Foscarini*, XVII c.

27c. Foscarini Chapel
Pietro Baratta, *Bust of Ludovico Foscarini*, XVII c.

27d. Foscarini Chapel
Pietro Groppelli, *Bust of Gerolamo Foscarini*, XVII c.

28. Francesco Migliori
Assunta, post 1722

29. Jacopo Amigoni
Saints Catherine and Andrew
1719

30. Gaetano Callido
and Family, *Organ*, 1772

The first church

The origins of a church dedicated to Saint Eustachius date from somewhere between the mid-tenth and early twelfth centuries, with 1127 being the first certain date. It had a nave and four aisle layout with exposed tie-beams and mosaic decorated chancel and apse. The façade looked onto salizzada di San Stae, the apses directly onto the *rio* of the same name and the left side onto a *campo* facing the Grand Canal. A chorus was probably built in the middle of the nave in the Gothic period and later demolished, while other significant alterations were made around the end of the sixteenth century.

The new church

In a state of severe dilapidation, the entire structure was demolished and rebuilt in 1678 by Giovanni Grassi, an otherwise completely unknown architect. He raised a completely different building: first and foremost it was rotated 90 degrees so as to face onto the *campo* and therefore the Grand Canal, turning its back on the quarter. The interior shows clear Palladian influences: the building is a *Saalkirche*, a single-hall, barrel-vaulted church with spacious, square chancel and three chapels on each side. These are separated by stout columns raised on high pedestals and support a strongly defined entablature. Large thermal windows make the church reasonably bright.

19. Giovanni Antonio Pellegrini
Crucifixion of St Andrew
1722-23

The façade

The cash legacy left by Doge Alvise II Mocenigo on his death in 1709 allowed a public competition to be staged for construction of the façade. It attracted various architects and was won by Domenico Rossi who, in 1710, built the façade and altars. The façade was also chosen according to a Palladian rather than Roman Baroque style: a simple order composed of four demi-columns on high pedestals supports a tympanum with small marble rose window in the centre and crowned with acroterial statues. The whole evokes the structure of an ancient temple, and is divided by a smaller order of Corinthian demi-columns with returned lesenes. This lesser order supports the tympanum divided by the arched doorway. The entablature continues over the lateral niches with statues between pairs of the main order. It is dominated by bas-relief decorated panels and ends in narrow wings corresponding to the lateral chapels inside, with demi-columns and returned lesenes, entablature and statue. The broken tympanum of the doorway, the upper statuary complex and the internal volutes represent a concession to Baroque art. The statues are the work of some of the most renowned sculptors of the time, including Torretto, Tarsi, Baratta, Cabianca, Groppelli and Corradini.

Chancel paintings

Another generous legacy, this time from Andrea Stazio, allowed the chancel to be decorated with canvases depicting the twelve apostles. These were all painted by different artists – novices and experienced experts – in avante garde Rococo and traditionalist styles, offering a pictorial anthology of the Venetian school in 1722. Pellegrini's *St Andrew* must have been the first of the series, representing as it does the client's patron saint. These were extremely busy months for the artist, who was then working on various paintings in Paris, Padua and Füssen representing saints such as Ulrich and Nicholas. It was therefore a renewal of religious themes which he was able to approach with all the experience and artistry he had accumulated over the years. In the masterful composition arranged on the diagonal, the contrast between light and shade offered a chance to portray the full drama of the martyrdom. In Giambattista Piazzetta's *St James the Great*, dated 1717 but also suggested as being around 1721, the naturalistic rhetoric of the gloomy Venetians is revived with a new impetus of feeling, resolved with new stylistic consistency. In the context of contemporary Venetian painting, the audacious simplicity of the work and its almost provocative realism contrasted both with the classicist academic school (Bambini, Lazzarini and Balestra), and with the elegance and pictorial creativity of the moderns (Ricci, Pellegrini and Pittoni). Referring to local seventeenth-century naturalism, and reforming it according to present needs of visual immediacy, Piazzetta restored an intensity of dramatic accent to the holy story aimed at the direct emotional involvement of the observer. The event is fixed at the moment of maximum tension, again, neither of the two characters stands out from the other. The old apostle, dishevelled and barefoot, grasping the soft parchment book, offers an extraordinary and unpredictable resistance, such as to unbalance the muscular executioner. In contrast with the coarse figures of the protagonists, a young, bright rider emerges in the background: an apparition of enigmatic elegance that speaks of the *Heads* of adolescents in which Piazzetta specialised. Right in front of Piazzetta's canvas, the *Martyrdom of St Bartholomew* by Giambattista Tiepolo seems in some respects its mirror image. The painting dates from 1722 when Tiepolo was twenty-six, and is typical of his early work, influenced by Piazzetta himself. The cruelty of the scene, the martyrdom of the saint being flayed alive after his capture in Armenia, is tremendous. The composition of the painting is created by the diverging movements of the saint and the executioner, in a precarious balance of contrasting forces. The old saint is in ecstasy, and there is no evident trace of strain in the fight between the two, all is resolved on the surface. The typolo-

10. Sebastiano Ricci
Liberation of St Peter, 1717-24

15. Giambattista Pittoni
Martyrdom of St Thomas
1722-23

17. Giambattista Piazzetta
St James the Great, 1717

9. **Giambattista Tiepolo**
Martyrdom of St Bartholomew
1722

gy of the 'old ecstatic' appears here for the first time, to reappear many times over the years, becoming one of the characteristic images of Tiepolo's religious painting (one example is in the San Polo altarpiece, *The Virgin appears to St John of Nepomuk*). There is an overall adherence to Baroque poetics in this painting, but he has already surpassed this, not only in the more accurate drawing, in total relief, but especially in the use of flaming colours. These light up the flesh and clothes, giving the scene drama and interest; the executioner's cap is illuminated with red and deep blue flashes, contrasted by the green hooded head of a youth at the bottom, stepping back with a gesture of horror, and once again easily identifiable as a portrait of Tiepolo himself.

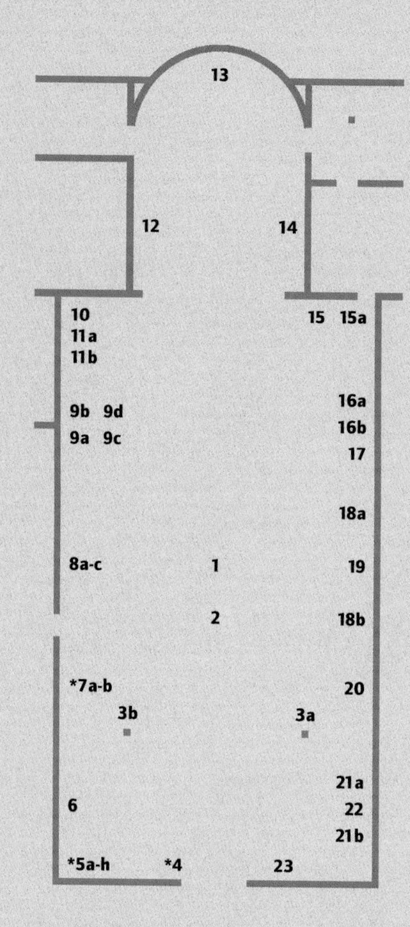

1. Ceiling
Pietro Antonio Torri
and Pietro Ricchi (attr.)
Architectural perspectives and figures, post 1674

2. *Renaissance gravestones on paving*

3a-b. Anonymous, XVI c.
- *Redeemer*
- *St John the Baptist*

***4.** Jacobello del Fiore (attr.)
Portrait of Father Philip
1420

***5a-h.** Lazzaro Bastiani (attr.), XV c.
- *Rachel at the Font*
- *Joseph found again*
- *The Golden Calf*
- *Joshua and the Taking of Jerico*
- *Solomon and the Queen of Sheba*
- *The Giant with Feet of Clay*
- *The Archangel Raphael and Tobius*
- *The Penury of Job*

6. Anonymous
Crucifix, XV c.

***7a-b.** Style of Jacopo Negretti called Palma Giovane, XVII c.
- *St Alvise*
- *St Augustine*

8a-c. Gian Maria Morlaiter (attr.), XVIII c.
- *St Dominic*
- *Virgin and Child*
- *St Theresa*

9a-d. School of Bonifacio de' Pitati, XVI c.
- *Announcing Angel*
- *Virgin Annunciata*
- *St Augustine*
- *St Alvise*

10. Stefano Paoluzzi
Adoration of the Sheperds
XVII c.

11a. Agostino Litterini (attr.)
St Anne with St Joseph and St Anthony of Padua
XVII c.

11b. Anonymous, *Christ carrying the Cross*, XVI c.

12. Chancel
Angelo Trevisani
Christ praying in the Olive Grove, XVII-XVIII c.

13. Chancel
Nicolò Moscatelli
Organ, 1760

14. Chancel
Giambattista Tiepolo
Ascent to Calvary, c. 1737-40

15. Stefano Paoluzzi
Adoration of the Magi
XVII c.

15a. Anonymous
Nun worshipping the Crucifix
XVII c.

16a-b. Giambattista Tiepolo
c. 1737-40
- *Crowning with Thorns*
- *Flagellation*

17. Girolamo da Santacroce (attr.), *Last Supper*, XVI c.

18a-b. Anonymous, XVI c.
- *St John the Baptist*
- *St Anthony*

19. Anonymous, *The Young Bishop Alvise*, XV c.

20. Pietro Damini (attr.)
St Louis consecrated Bishop of Toulouse, XVII c.

21a-b. Pietro Muttoni called Pietro della Vecchia, XVII c.
- *The Saracens refuse to inspect the Basket containing the Body of St Mark*
- *Purloining the Body of St Mark*

22. Antonio Zanchi
The Redeemer with St Peter and St Paul, XVII c.

23. Anonymous after Paolo Caliari called Veronese
Supper in the House of the Pharisee, XVII c.

Origins

The northern part of the city, made up of long, narrow islands between parallel canals, was created by the reclamation and artificial solidification of sandbanks and shallows which began in the first years of the Republic. Once rich in parks and vegetable gardens, this is still a fascinating area lying solitary and remote on the margins of the lagoon.
It is said that St Louis, Bishop of Toulouse, appeared in a dream to the patrician Antonia Venier, persuading her to build a convent in his honour; in any case, the foundations of the monastery were laid in 1388. Tradition has it that Venier then retired to a monastic life there following the Order of St Augustine.

The building

The Gothic church, now in exposed brick, has a simple, single-nave basilica layout, with large square, apsidal chancel. The façade is divided by six lesenes and crowned by suspended arches, with sloped central section and flat sides; the only decorations are a central oeil-deboeuf and Gothic doorway in Istrian stone, with a fifteenth century statue of St Louis in the lunette. Above the entrance is one of the first Venetian examples of a hanging choir, for the nuns of the attached convent. The *barco* (nun's gallery) rests on two columns with fifteenth-century buttresses and capitals. It has undergone various modifications in appearance; its large windows with wrought iron gratings are from the eighteenth century. The interior was the object of numerous changes as early as the seventeenth century, with the addition of altars, marbles and sculptures, but mainly with construction of the plain ceiling, frescoed in false architectural perspective that seems to break through the roof. This was completed towards the end of the century by Pietro Antonio Torri and Pietro Ricchi. It is quite charming, but clashes somewhat with the overall Gothic style.

Christ's Passion

Three canvases depicting *Christ's Passion*, commissioned from Giambattista Tiepolo by the patrician Alvise Cornaro, hang in the chancel and nave. The *Crowning with Thorns*, the *Flagellation* and the *Ascent to Calvary*, were originally part of a tryptych, now separated; the first two hang on the right of the nave and the third in the chancel. Painted around 1737-40, they are subsequent to the frescoes in the church of the Gesuati.
The Sant'Alvise works are notable both for their composition and colouring. The central canvas, hung in the chancel, is without doubt the most openly dramatic. In representing Christ bent under the weight of the cross, Tiepolo created an entire parade of people; the scene is animated, sumptuous and of great tragic effect. Its composition was in-

21b. Pietro Muttoni called Pietro della Vecchia
Purloining the Body of St Mark
XVII c.

14. Giambattista Tiepolo
Ascent to Calvary, c. 1737-40

1. Pietro Antonio Torri and Pietro Ricchi (attr.)
Ceiling with architectural perspectives and figures, post 1674

spired by the grandiosity and luminist dynamism of Tintoretto, but there are also other sources: such as in the choice of Biblical personalities from Rembrandt's engravings, which Tiepolo was familiar with thanks to the collection owned by his friend Anton Maria Zanetti. The prostrate body of Christ is touching and rich in fascination, but the emphasis on the red of his robe is regarded by some as making it rather too pathetic. The cross he carries is enormous and over-long; it is scenographic, as are the expressions of suffering and the contorted position of the body. Both the *Crowning* and the *Flagellation* unfold on a background of architecture, introduced by short stairways, with groups of figures observing the scene. In both cases, the suffering figure of Christ stands out against the background and is of great emotional impact. In that period the artist was highly attracted to theatre in costume and drew inspiration from the scenery of the many melodramas staged all over the city.

5d.-5b. Lazzaro Bastiani (attr.)
Joshua and the Taking of Jerico
Joseph found again, XV c.

Biblical stories

Eight small panels depicting episodes from the Old Testament are housed on the inside of the façade, originally from the no longer extant church of Santa Maria delle Vergini.
These works had a period of popularity between the mid-nineteenth and early twentieth centuries, possibly because of their naïve simplicity recalling the manner of pre-sixteenth-century artists, and were even attributed to the early work of Vittore Carpaccio. It now seems rather more correct to suggest Lazzaro Bastiani on the basis of ideas expressed by contemporary critics. The narrative openness and graphic severity, still marked by a Mantegna influence, which typify his more important works seem to place it closer to this artist. Here the slightly immature charm of the drawing and the colours tending towards dull tones would place Bastiani amongst the latecomers who, although working in the late fifteenth century, had not yet renewed their palettes according to the example of the more advanced masters, such as the Bellini.

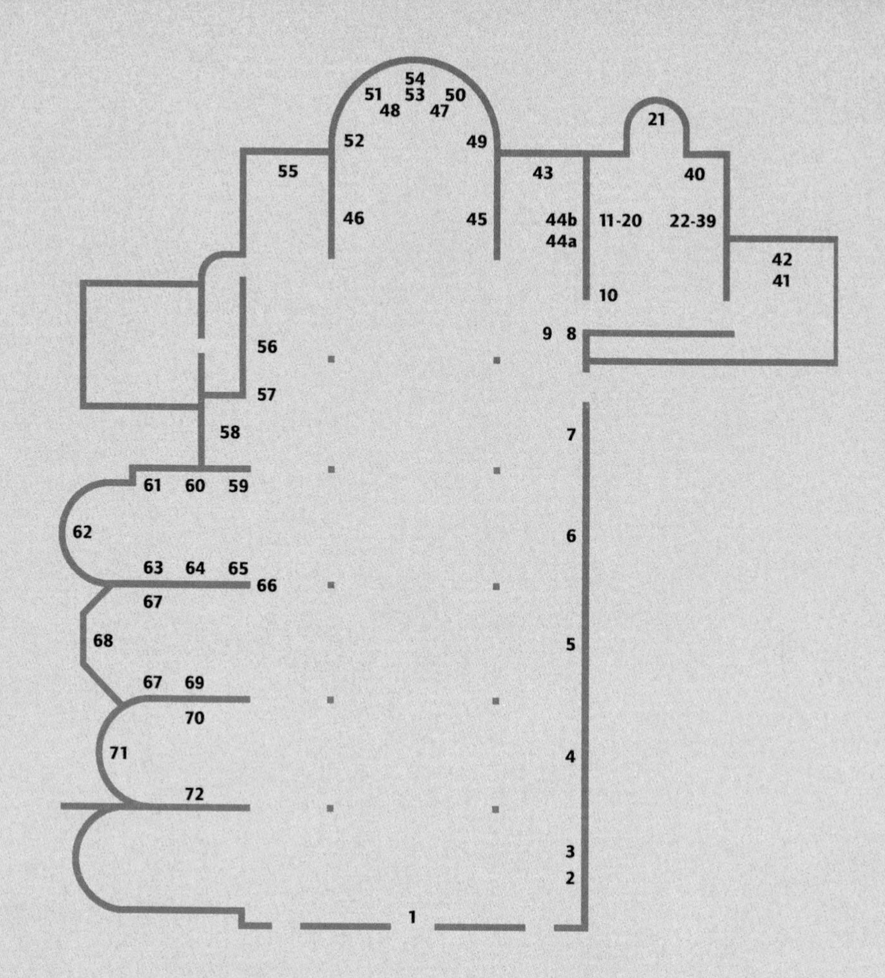
54
51 53 50
48 47
21
52 49
55 43 40
46 45 44b 11-20 22-39
44a
42
41
10
9 8
56
57
58 7
61 60 59
62 6
63 64 65
66
67
68 5
67 69
70
71 4
72
3
2
1

1. Pietro Bazzani, *Organ*, 1878

2. Antonio Rizzo (attr.)
Virgin and Child, XV c.

3. Giambattista Cima da Conegliano
St John the Baptist with Saints Peter, Mark, Jerome and Paul
c. 1495

4. Copy after Giambattista Cima da Conegliano (workshop)
St Christopher, XIX c.

5. Anonymous, *Virgin*, c. 1870

6. Giuseppe Sardi, Francesco Cavrioli, Giusto Le Court
Monument to Girolamo Cavazza, 1675

7. Daniel van den Dyck
Martyrdom of St Laurence
XVII c.

8. Giovanni De Santi
Virgin and Child, XIV c.

9. Jacopo Robusti called Tintoretto
Presentation of the Virgin at the Temple, 1552-53

10. St Mauro's Chapel
Copy after Gerolamo Savoldo
Lament over the Dead Christ
XVII c.

11-20. St Mauro's Chapel
Various artists, *Venetian Saints and Blessed*, XVII c.

21. St Mauro's Chapel
Antonio Molinari
Virgin and Child to whom St Mauro Abbot recommends a Couple of Worshippers
XVII c.

22-39. St Mauro's Chapel
Various artists, *Venetian Saints and Blessed*, XVII c.

40. St Mauro's Chapel
Giovanni De Santi
Madonna dell'Orto, 1377

41. Sacristy
Washbasin, XV c.

42. Sacristy
School of Paris Bordone
Virgin and Child with Saints
XVI-XVII c.

43. Chapel of Tintoretto
Girolamo Santacroce
Saints Augustine and Jerome
XVI c.

44a. Chapel of Tintoretto
Tomb of Jacopo Robusti called Tintoretto and family
1863

44b. Chapel of Tintoretto
Napoleone Martinuzzi
Bust of Tintoretto, 1937

45-52. Chancel
Jacopo Robusti called Tintoretto
- *Last Judgement*, c. 1562-63
- *Adoration of the Golden Calf* c. 1562-63
- *Beheading of St Paul* c. 1556
- *Apparition of the Cross to St Peter*, c. 1556
- *Strenght*, c. 1562-63
- *Prudence*, c. 1562-63
- *Justice*, c. 1562-63
- *Temperance*, c. 1562-63

53. Chancel
Jacopo Negretti called Palma Giovane
Annunciation, 1596-1605

54. Chancel
Pietro Ricchi, *Faith*, XVII c.

55. Copy after Giovanni Antonio de Sacchis called Pordenone
The Blessed Laurence Giustiniani, Saints and Two Canons of San Giorgio in Alga, XIX c.

56. Matteo Ponzone
St George with Saints Jerome and Trifone, XVII c.

57. Domenico Tintoretto
Holy Father in Glory, c. 1590

58. Matteo Ponzone
Flagellation of Christ, XVII c.

59. Contarini Chapel
Bust of Alvise Contarini
(† 1651)

60. Contarini Chapel
Alessandro Vittoria
Bust of Tommaso Contarini
(† 1578)

61. Contarini Chapel
Bust of Tommaso Contarini
(† 1614)

62. Contarini Chapel
Jacopo Robusti called Tintoretto, *Miracle of St Agnes*, c. 1577

63. Contarini Chapel
Bust of Alvise Contarini
(† 1579)

64. Contarini Chapel
Danese Cattaneo, *Bust of Gasparo Contarini*, c. 1563

65. Contarini Chapel
Bust of Carlo Contarini
(† 1688)

66. Follower of Titian
Virgin and Child with Saints
XVI c.

67-68. Morosini Chapel
Domenico Tintoretto
- *Angel censers*, XVII c.
- *Nativity*, c. 1625-30

69. Morosini Chapel
Jacopo Negretti called Palma Giovane
Crucifixion, c. 1579-80

70. Vendramin Chapel
Jacopo Negretti called Palma Vecchio, *St Vincent Martyr with St Dominic, Pope Eugene IV, the Blessed Laurence Giustiniani and St Helen*
1523-24

71. Vendramin Chapel
Bartolomeo Litterini
Dead Christ received by the Holy Father and the Holy Spirit, Our Lady of Sorrows and St John of Matha, 1708

72. Tiziano Vecellio
Tobius and the Angel
c. 1540-45

Site and origins

The Madonna dell'Orto church is on the northernmost edge of the city. It faces onto the *campo* of the same name, one of the last in Venice to retain its original herring-bone terracotta paving between squares of Istrian stone, in which San Marco's square was once also paved. The Scuola di San Cristoforo, called dei Mercanti, is on the west side of the *campo*. This was a busy commercial and mercantile area from the fourteenth century as it was the main approach for traffic crossing the northern lagoon between the islands and the mainland. So it was no mere chance that the church was dedicated to St Christopher, patron saint of boatmen, pilgrims, travellers and merchants. Martyred in Lycia during persecutions by the Emperor Decius in the third century, he became the subject of various legends. The most well-known is the one in the *Legenda aurea* by Jacopo da Varagine. Here he is represented as a giant who, in search of the most powerful king in the world, eventually discovers Christ and puts himself at his service. He settles on the banks of a river where he ferries wayfarers as an act of charity. One evening, the weight of a boy he is carrying increases until he can no longer bear it: the boy then reveals himself as his king and the creator of the world, and tells him to plant his stick in the ground, which will flower the day after. The name Christopher actually means 'carrier of Christ', and the most usual iconography shows him with the stick of the legend. However, an impressive Virgin and Child sculpted in soft stone by Giovanni De Santi, which had been kept in the garden since the foundation of the church, gradually became an object of pilgrimage as it was deemed to have miraculous powers. It was therefore moved into the church which consequently took on its new name. The building was more or less completed in 1377, but by 1399 was already in need of serious and lengthy restoration; other works were carried out in 1473 and the doorway completed in 1483.

Detail of the façade

The religious orders

It is also understandable how the foundation of the church was owed to the Order of the Umiliati. This was derived from a paupers' movement that had sprung up amongst wool workers in Lombard cities at the end of the twelfth century. It brought religious commitment and economics together in the processing and selling of wool, working to develop the centres in which it was established. However, by the fifteenth century the Venetian community was already showing irreversible signs of decay, losing credibility and authority among the faithful, and was

47. Jacopo Robusti called Tintoretto
Beheading of St Paul, c. 1556
detail

therefore replaced in 1461 by the secular canons of San Giorgio in Alga, under whom the church reached its maximum artistic splendour, reflecting an intense spiritual life. The congregation, which arose on the initiative of a small group of young Venetian nobles, was committed to restoration of the church buildings, the daily celebration of the faith and residence of the faithful in the community.

Façade

The façade, in exposed brick, reflects the church's internal tripartition, with a high central sloping section and two lower side sections, enclosed by four buttresses. It is rich in decorative elements in Istrian stone, red Verona marble, terracotta and porphyry: statues, niches, aediculae, hanging arches, friezes, two large ogee windows, a rose window, an oeil-de-boeuf and, in particular, the doorway. Statues of the Apostles stand on the galleries crowning the lateral slopes, while there are sculptures of the Virtues in the five upper shrines. The latter were placed there towards the middle of the nineteenth century and came from Santo Stefano in Murano. The doorway may have been designed by Bartolomeo Bon. It is an extremely elegant mesh of Gothic and Renaissance elements, and directly introduces the church's dual dedication: the statues that crown it being of St Christopher in the centre and the Virgin announced by the Archangel Gabriel at the sides.

47. Jacopo Robusti called Tintoretto
Beheading of St Paul, c. 1556

Interior

The church has a basilica layout with nave and aisles separated by six large ogee arches on Greek marble columns with matching capitals, ending in a chancel with polygon apse and two small rectangular chapels. Four altars are arranged along the right wall, next to the cloister, while four deep chapels and access to the bell tower open up on the left. In the nineteen-thirties the wooden lacunar ceiling, flat over the nave and sloping over the aisles, was added and the frescoes decorating the intrados above nave and aisles restored.

Jacopo Robusti called Tintoretto

Madonna dell'Orto houses the canvases painted over a thirty year period by Jacopo Robusti, called Tintoretto (1519-94). The artist lived near the church at number 3399, and was buried here, along with his son and daughter, Domenico and Marietta, and father in law, in a kind of family pantheon. Tintoretto worked in Madonna dell'Orto for the first time between 1552 and 1553, decorating the external doors of the organ, then on the right of the chancel, with the *Presentation of the Virgin at the Temple*. The canvases have now been reunited. His model for the work was Titian's *Presentation at the Temple* of 1537 – now in the Gallerie dell'Accademia – but that paratactical composition in which the eye reaches the little Mary passing from person to person, almost following the rustling and animation of the crowd, is here completely surpassed. The staircase, and the cusp of the pyramid at its summit, lead the eye straight to the meeting between Mary and the uppermost priest; then, little by little, the figures arranged on the steps emerge from shadow and silence. A light source outside the painting supplements the weak light glimpsed on the horizon to shape the groups of women in the foreground. The figurative whole of the doors is fundamental to understanding Tintoretto's use of space: a space that no longer opens up at right angles to the viewer, as in the Renaissance conception, but creates images beyond the edge of the picture, or rises to a precipice blocking the perspective opening. The light-shade opposition separated the two doors with a clear symbolic value, distinguishing the world beyond Grace from that in Grace. On the left, immersed in darkness, are those Jews who would not accept conversion; on the right the light illuminates those who believe, represented by three female groups of mothers with children. Now imagine the doors opening up: inside, too, the ultimate expedient for the logical construction of space – architecture – has been surpassed. The dark atmosphere of the *Presentation* unfolds to give precedence to the light of which the martyrs are part: the *Beheading of St Paul* and the *Apparition of the Cross to St Peter*, painted in 1556 circa, now kept in the chancel. The apostles, the two pillars of the new Temple – the Church – correspond to the image of Mary, Temple of Christ. In the historical-religious context of those years, when there were also demonstrations of sympathy for the Protestant Reformation in Venice, these images seem to take on the value of a response to the Lutheran position on the authority of Church and pope. Right from its very beginnings, the Alga community was part of that wide movement for Catholic reform that hoped for the radical renewal of the Church, but renewal that came from within and was guided by papal authority. The two canvases confirm the authority of the Church and allude also to the theme of the justification to be found in Grace, but also through works – primarily martyrdom, the full imitation of Christ, and participation in his work of saving – as opposed to the Protestant theory of predestination.

48. Jacopo Robusti called Tintoretto
Apparition of the Cross to St Peter, c. 1556

Tintoretto probably worked on the two cuspidal canvases for the apse in 1562-63. It is said that he was awarded the prestigious commission by offering his work in exchange for the cost of materials alone, wishing to demonstrate to all and to himself that he was able to work out a composition in a space fourteen metres high and six wide. The impetus of his imagination and narrative enthusiasm can be appreciated in both paintings, but these are kept in check by the experience of a wise director who knows how to measure light and shade, and to multiply the subjects without renouncing the pleasure of description. The formal elegance of the figures is caught in the *Adoration of the Golden Calf.* Its theme of the unfaithfulness of the chosen people also prefigures the sins of the Christians, and is faced on the opposite wall by the New Testament version in the *Last Judgement.* Here there are not several episodes to be narrated; the protagonist is motion. A whirling motion involving angels and the damned, comprising bodies in bold poses and torsions that saturate the space almost as if, despite their enormous size, the canvases were still not large enough to completely stage the event overwhelming men and things. In the *Judgement* not only is the divine justice which punishes depicted, but also that which redeems and saves those who believe in Christ. The presence of Charity, at the head of the line of the elect, nevertheless highlights the value of works

9. Jacopo Robusti called Tintoretto
Presentation of the Virgin at the Temple, 1552-53

in the plan of salvation. Jacopo finished decorating the apse in the same years with paintings of the four cardinal *Virtues*: *Temperance*, *Justice*, *Prudence* and *Strength*. These are represented as feminine figures recognisable by their respective symbols: *Temperance* has two jugs, to 'temper' the wine with water or cold water with hot; *Justice* carries a sword and scales; *Prudence* holds a snake, in conformance with the words in the Gospel of Matthew 'be prudent like snakes', and a compass, which gives the measure of all things; finally, *Strength* rests on a broken column, recalling King Solomon in the Book of Judges. On a doctrinal level they are decisive because they address human behaviour towards the good, concentrated in works. These too, therefore, seem to echo the Catholic argument against Lutheran doctrine which gave little consideration to moral virtues in the life of the Christian as a means to salvation. Tintoretto returned to the Madonna dell'Orto around 1577 to carry out his last work, the altarpiece with the *Miracle of St Agnes* for the Contarini Chapel. The saint is the focal point of the composition, shining with her own light in a slightly off-centre position. Surprise is registered by the bystanders nearest her: the group on the right and the Roman prefect. The latter is in imaginative clothing of a deep red that contrasts with the figure of the raised youth in the foreground. Behind the crowd, which seems to comment on the event in amazement, white columns suggesting Roman buildings arise and connect the lower part of the painting to the upper, where angels bear the martyr's crown. Their deep blue clothes could connote the colour of those worn by the secular canons of San Giorgio in Alga. The psychological study of the characters and the crowd is 'modern', carried out with elements of mannerist language, which may be compared with the *Presentation of the Virgin at the Temple* of ten years earlier on the opposite wall of the nave.

Giambattista Cima da Conegliano

Cima da Conegliano probably painted the panel showing *St John the Baptist with Saints Peter, Mark, Jerome and Paul* for the Saraceno Altar between 1493 and 1495. This is an example of the perfect integration of illusory and real space: the painted architecture joins with and ends in the sculpted architecture of the frame. This brings it into relation with the overall church architecture, repeating columns similar to those in the nave and choosing an asymmetrical arrangement of the painted architecture for the altarpiece of this corner altar, which, taking nothing from the front view, creates a perspective particularly favourable to an oblique view of the nave. The Baptist turns his head towards the light coming from the large window in the façade, a gesture that helps accentuate the communication between the two worlds: the religious world of the painting and the earthly one of the Church. The extremely complicated iconography of the altarpiece, which interprets the ideal of holiness concentrated in scorn for things of the world, was certainly the result of direct intervention on the part of the secular canons of San Giorgio in Alga. A classical doorway in ruins is brought up to date in a Venetian sense by the variety of capitals and the marble of the columns,

45. Jacopo Robusti called Tintoretto
Last Judgement, c. 1562-63

62. Jacopo Robusti called Tintoretto
Miracle of St Agnes, c. 1577

by the mosaic decoration of the pendentives and by the tie-beam reinforcing the arches. It represents the ancient world destined to disappear with the coming of Christ. Thriving plants such as ivy and figs grow out of the ruins, the latter being regarded as the symbol of the tree of the Cross and therefore protection against all evil, corporal and spiritual. An owl is perched on the ruins, in line with the figure of the Baptist, conveying numerous symbolic meanings. It is probably an allusion to the prophetic role of the precursor, shown at the centre on a pedestal, who combines ascetic discipline with the declaration of sins and an invitation to conversion. Saints Peter and Mark on the left and Paul and Jerome on the right represent the Church which, through the closed book – the knowledge set down in the Scriptures – knows and teaches what is necessary for the salvation of man.

San Pietro di Castello

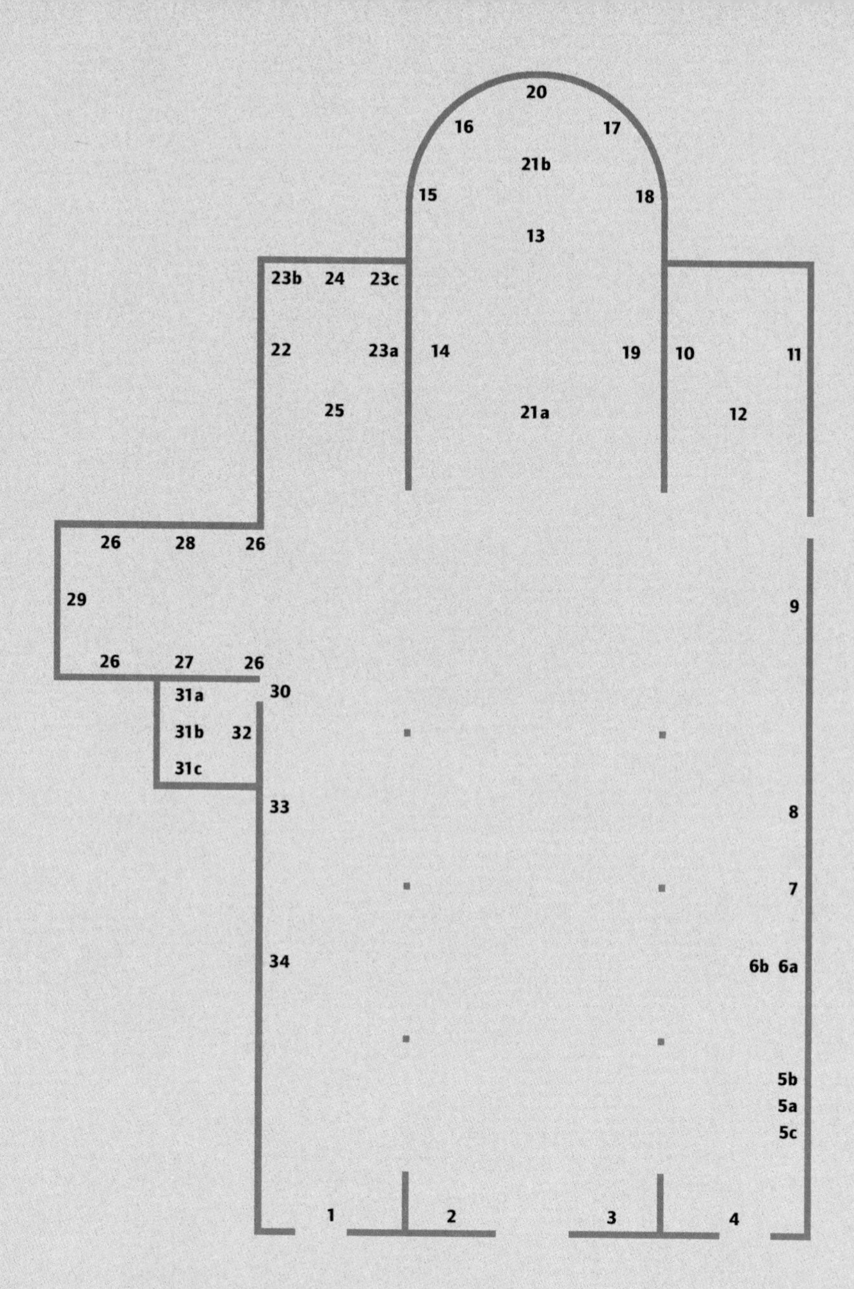

1. Copy after Marco Basaiti
St George and the Princess
XIX c.

2. Pietro Malombra
and Antonio Vassillacchi
called Aliense, *Supper at Emmaus* (or *Feast of the Jewish Passover*), c. 1618

3. Anonymous and Jacopo Beltrame (attr.), *Supper in Simon's House*, XVI c.

4. Anonymous
Burial urn of Procurator Filippo Correr († 1417)

5a. Jacopo Spada (attr.)
Crucifix, XVIII c.

5b-c. Orazio Marinali (attr.)
XVIII c.
- *Faith*
- *Contemplation*

6a. Tiziano Vecellio
called Tizianello (attr.)
Holy Father in Glory, XVII c.

6b. Anonymous, Byzantine
Virgin and Child, XIII c.

7. Islamic art
St Peter's Throne, marble chair from Antioch, XIII c.

8. Marco Basaiti
St Peter Enthroned and four Saints, XVI c.

9. Francesco Ruschi
Virgin with Saints Helen, Thomas the Apostle and Francis, 1640

10. Right Chapel
Pietro Ricchi, *Adoration of the Magi*, c. 1662

11. Right Chapel
Pietro Liberi, *Chastising the Serpent*, c. 1660

12. ceiling of the Right Chapel
Pietro Ricchi (attr.)
The Sons of Jacob sent to Egypt to buy Grain recognised by Joseph, c. 1650

13. Chancel
Francesco Cavrioli, Giusto Le Court, Melchior Barthel, Clemente Moli, on drawing by Baldassarre Longhena
Main altar, 1649

14. Chancel
Gregorio Lazzarini, *Charity of St Laurence Giustiniani*, 1691

15. Chancel
Antonio Molinari
St Laurence Giustiniani frees One Possessed, c. 1695

16. Chancel
Daniel Heinz, *Baby Jesus appears to St Laurence Giustiniani*, c. 1695

17. Chancel
Domenico Ghislandi (attr.)
St Laurence Giustiniani administers Holy Communion to a Nun, XVII c.

18. Chancel
Giovanni Segala, *Death of St Laurence Giustiniani*
c. 1695

19. Chancel
Antonio Bellucci
St Laurence Giustiniani intercedes to free Venice from the Plague of 1447, 1695

20. Chancel
Pietro Nacchini, *Organ*, 1754

21a. Chancel Vault
Girolamo Pellegrini
Glory of the Holy Trinity
c. 1695

21b. Basin of the apse
Girolamo Pellegrini
Glory of St Laurence Giustiniani, c. 1695

22. Chapel of the Cross
Francesco Solimena (attr.)
The Invention of the Cross
XVIII c.

23a-c. Chapel of the Cross
Veneto School and Francesco Solimena (attr.), XVIII c.
- *Glorification of the Cross*
- *The Virgin and Mary Magdalene*
- *St John the Evangelist*

24. Chapel of the Cross
Anonymous, *Copper Cross*
XIV-XVIII c.

25. ceiling of the Chapel of the Cross
Anonymous, *Glory of St Charles Borromeo*, XVII c.

Vendramin Chapel
Michele Ungaro on drawing by Baldassarre Longhena, XVII c.

26. Vendramin Chapel
Melchior Barthel or Michele Ungaro and assistants
Allegorical statues, 1675

27. Vendramin Chapel
School of Michele Ungaro
Triumph of the Cross, c. 1675

28. Vendramin Chapel
Michele Ungaro, *Paul V assigns the Cardinal's Hat to Francesco Vendramin*, c. 1675

29. Vendramin Chapel
Luca Giordano, *Virgin and Child with Souls in Purgatory*
c. 1650

30. Paolo Caliari
called Veronese
Saints John the Evangelist, Peter and Paul, 1585-88

31a. Lando Chapel
Arminio Zuccato, *Glory of the Saints*, on cartoon by Jacopo Robusti called Tintoretto, 1570

31b. Lando Chapel
Anonymous, *Marble pluteus* altar frontal, IX c.

31c. Lando Chapel
Anonymous, *Fragment of late Roman mosaic*, V c.

32. Lando Chapel
Anonymous, *Bust of St Laurence Giustiniani*, XV c.

33. Gian Maria Morlaiter
Immacolata, XVIII c.

34. Alessandro Varotari
called Padovanino
with adaptations by Michelangelo Schiavoni
Martyrdom of St John the Evangelist, XVII c.

Façade

7. Islamic art
St Peter's Throne, marble chair from Antioch, XIII c.

Michele Ungaro on drawing by Baldassarre Longhena
Vendramin Chapel, XVII c.

Origins

The island of Olivolo was the easternmost part of the city until the later creation of Sant'Elena. Separated from the urban context by a wide canal, it still retains the atmosphere of peace and isolation it has enjoyed since the first settlements were made in the fifth and sixth centuries. There was apparently a church here dedicated to Saints Sergio and Bacchus in the seventh century, presumably sited near a defensive castle that gave the whole sestiere its name, while the first building dedicated to St Peter dates from the mid ninth century. Olivolo was a bishop's see from 775 in competition with the nearby patriarchal seat of Grado, until 1451 when Pope Nicholas V put an end to the argument by uniting the two episcopal sees and creating the patriarchate of Venice. San Pietro di Castello was then the city's cathedral until 1807 when, the Republic having fallen, the title was transferred to San Marco's, until then the Doge's chapel. The first patriach of Venice, the Blessed Laurence Giustiniani, is buried beneath the main altar.

The new church

The old church obviously underwent restorations and reconstruction work over the centuries. Then, in 1559, the Patriarch Vincenzo Diedo commissioned Andrea Palladio to rebuild the cathedral, but work was interrupted at the end of the same year by the death of the patriarch.

The façade

The façade was built between 1594-96 by Francesco Smeraldi, who had had the opportunity to work with Palladio and probably faithfully followed his directions, or at least his lessons. The façade is divided into three, echoing the interior layout. The higher central section is marked by four Composite demi-columns on high pedestals and crowned by a tympanum; it is almost entirely taken up by the doorway, framed with Corinthian lesenes, festoons and another tympanum. The lesenes are taken up again on the side wings, which have similar doorways but of smaller size and festoons of the same height as the central one. They are completed by those fragments of tympanum typical of Palladian churches, alluding to the intersection of a second temple façade behind the main one.

The interior

The main body of the church was rebuilt beginning in 1619 by Giangirolamo Grapiglia under the patriarchate of Giovanni III Tiepolo. The layout is a Latin cross with nave and aisles and non-projecting transept, square chancel and semicircular apse with two rectangular chapels alongside. A side chapel built subsequently by Baldassarre Longhena prolongs the left arm of the transept. The nave and aisles are cross vaulted, while the transept and apses are barrel vaulted and the crossing domed. With an altar in each span of the aisles, and the spans clearly marked by the cross vaulting and by pillars and pilasters, the aisles lose the effect of spatial continuity and presage the custom of placing chapels in rows.
The church is extremely bright, with the darker parts being those set aside for prayer.

St Peter's Throne

There was always veiled competition between San Pietro, at the very edge of the city, and San Marco, at its physical and political heart, the symbol of spiritual and temporal power, of the papacy and the Serenissima. And to this corresponded the throne of St Mark displayed for public devotion in San Marco and the presumed throne of St Peter, originally kept in the chancel of the cathedral. This quite notable work was a gift to the Doge from the Eastern Emperor Michael III (842-67), and has stood next to the right wall since 1752. It is certainly a composite creation. The front section may be made up of the remains of a bishops throne, but the dossal is an important Near East bas-relief of the Seljuk period, probably from around the mid-eleventh century, decorated with tendrils, floral and astral motifs and an epigraphic text.

The main altar

In line with the increasing public veneration for the Blessed Laurence Giustiniani, work was begun in 1646 to rebuild the main altar to hold his remains, to a design by Baldassarre Longhena with sculptures by Francesco Cavrioli, Giusto Le Court, Melchior Barthel and Clemente Moli. The polychrome marble structure, scenically animated as much in its design as its plastic decoration created a new figurative focus in the chancel, underlining the Saint's function of intercession between the Divinity and the Republic of which he had been both patrician and first patriarch.

8. Marco Basaiti
St Peter Enthroned and four Saints, XVI c.

29. Luca Giordano
Virgin and Child with Souls in Purgatory, c. 1650

The Vendramin and Lando Chapels

The Vendramin Chapel opens out from the left arm of the transept, dedicated to Our Lady of Carmine to celebrate the Patriarch Francesco Vendramin. It is decorated with distinguished seventeenth century designs by Baldassarre Longhena and enriched by the sculpture and bas-reliefs of Michele Ungaro, all culminating in the lovely altarpiece by Luca Giordano (1650 c.) depicting the *Virgin and Child with Souls in Purgatory*. Alongside is the small Lando Chapel, whose Gothic style proclaims origins dating from the building preceding the current one. The altar bears a mosaic altarpiece by Zuccato on a cartoon by Tintoretto, while a significant fragment of mosaic at the base of the altar is testimony to the ancient traditions of the church.

The bell tower

The bell tower rises separately from the church and is quite special. It was rebuilt between 1482-90 by Mauro Codussi, not in brick but with a facing of Istrian stone, and so constitutes one of the first early Renaissance works in Venice. The dome was replaced with a polygonal drum in 1670.

Santissimo Redentore

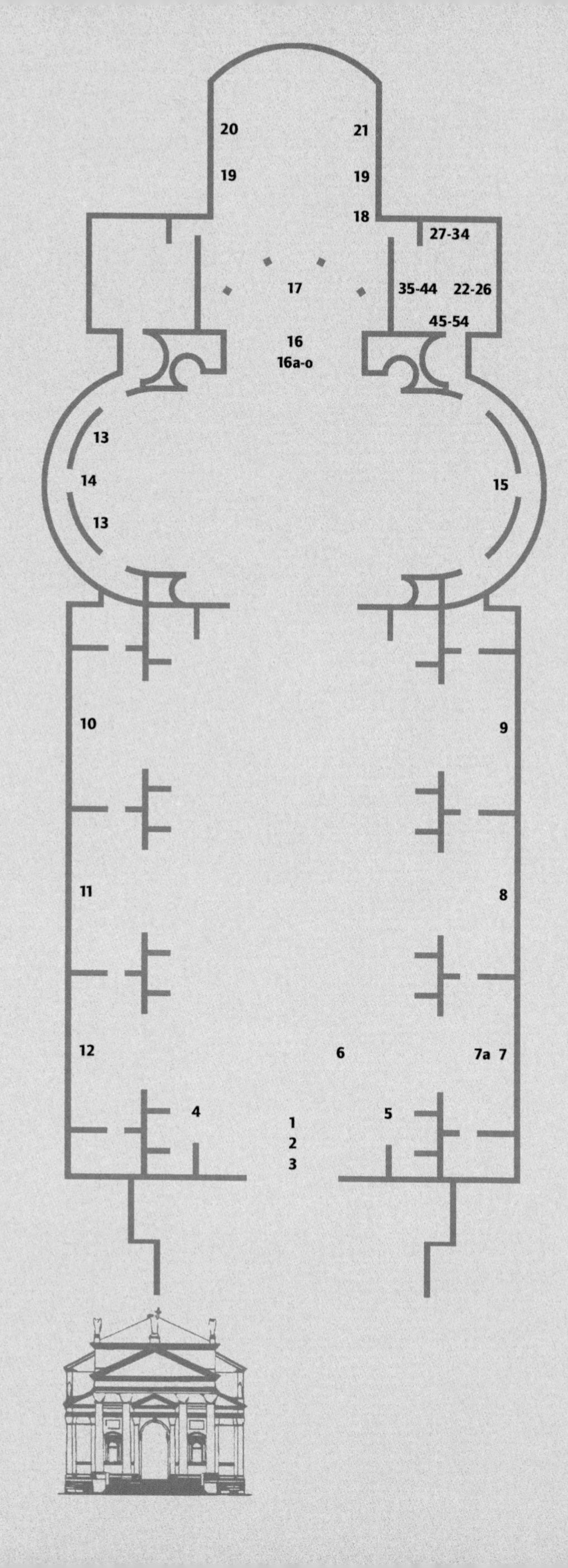

1. Paolo Piazza
Venice's Votive Offering for Liberation from the Plague of 1575-77, 1619

2. *Marble stone* commemorating the 1576 votive offering for the liberation of Venice from the plague

3. Pietro Muttoni called Pietro della Vecchia
St Felix of Cantalice receives the Baby Jesus from the Virgin, XVII c.

4-5. Francesco Terilli
- *Marble stoup with St John the Baptist*, 1610
- *Marble stoup with the Redeemer*, XVII c.

6. Veneto cabinet-maker
Crucifix, XVII c.

7. Francesco Bassano
Birth of Christ, XVI c.

7a. Fortunato Arnaldi
Stories of Mary and Christ altar frontal, 1835

8. Successors of Paolo Caliari called Veronese
Baptism of Christ, XVI c.

9. Domenico Tintoretto
Flagellation of Christ, c. 1588

10. Jacopo Negretti called Palma Giovane
Transport of Christ to the Sepulchre, c. 1600

11. Francesco Bassano
Resurrection of Christ, XVI c.

12. Domenico Tintoretto
Ascension of Christ, c. 1588

13. *Series of four kneeling stools*, XVI c.

14. *Chair*, reserved for the Doge during the ceremony of the Redentore, XVII-XVIII c.

15. Ruffatti Company
Organ, 1955

16. *Main altar*, 1680

16a-c. Gerolamo Campagna 1590
- *Crucifix*
- *St Mark*
- *St Francis*

16d-i. Giuseppe Mazza 1705-07
- *Six Angels with the Instruments of the Passion*
- *St Sebastian*
- *St Roch*
- *Four Doctors of the Church*
- *St Peter*
- *St Paul*

16l-o. Tommaso Rues, 1682
- *Trinity*
- *Christ praying in the Olive Grove*
- *Ascent to Calvary*, altar frontal
- *Deposition from the Cross* bas-relief on back of altar

17. Tommaso Rues, 1682
Blessed Redeemer, XVIII c.

18. Francesco Fontebasso (attr.), Father *Marco d'Aviano with the Faithful*, XVIII c.

19. *High-backed chairs* XVIII c.

20. Veneto painter
St Francis receives the Stigmata, XVI-XVII c.

21. Veneto painter
Christ praying in the Olive Grove, XVI-XVII c.

22. Sacristy
Veneto circle, *The Archangel Raphael with Tobius*, XVI c.

23. Sacristy
Follower of Jacopo Negretti called Palma Giovane
Christ supported by Angels XVI-XVII c.

24. Sacristy
Veneto circle, *The Archangel Michael*, XVII c.

25. Sacristy
Brother Francesco Maria da Vicenza, *Architectural reliquary*, XIX c.

26. Sacristy
Monastic craft
Reliquares with faces of Capucins Saints, XIX c.

27. Sacristy
Veneto circle, *Lament over the Dead Christ*, XVII c.

28. Sacristy
Our Lady of Sorrows with Crucifix, icon, XVII c.

29. Sacristy
Our Lady of Consolation icon, XVI-XVII c.

30. Sacristy
Jacopo Tatti called Sansovino (attr.), *Virgin and Child*, XVI c.

31. Sacristy
Domenico Corvi, *Ecstasy of St Laurence of Brindisi*, 1785

32. Sacristy
Carlo Saraceni, *Ecstasy of St Francis*, 1620

33a-d. Sacristy
Follower of Francesco Bassano, XVI c.
- *The Fall of Manna*
- *The Loaves of the Proposition*
- *Last Supper*
- *Supper at Emmaus*

34. Sacristy
Reliquary with the Cloak of St Laurence of Brindisi XVIII c.

35. Sacristy
Copy after Francesco Bassano
Deposition, XVII c.

36. Sacristy
Crucifixes, XVII c.

37. Sacristy
Copy after Jacopo da Ponte called Jacopo Bassano
Transport of Christ, XVII c.

38. Sacristy
Circle of Francesco Bassano
Resurrection, XVI c.

39. Sacristy
Northern sphere
Holy Face, XVII c.

40. Sacristy
Follower of Bassanos
Flagellation, XVII c.

41-43. Sacristy
Architectural reliquaries with armed reliquaries XVII-XVIII c.

42. Sacristy
Alvise Vivarini
Virgin and Child with Two Musician Angels, c. 1500

44. Sacristy
Wooden Crucifix with *Four Evangelists* and two *ampullae*

45. Sacristy
Paolo Caliari called Veronese
Baptism of Christ, c. 1561

46. Sacristy
Jacopo Negretti called Palma Giovane
Virgin and Child with the Infant St John and Saints Jerome, Anne, Francis and Catherine of Alexandria c. 1581

47. Sacristy
Francesco Bissolo
Virgin and Child with Saints John the Evangelist and Catherine of Alexandria XVI c.

48. Sacristy
Circle of Jacopo Negretti called Palma Giovane
Our Lady of Sorrows XVI-XVII c.

49. Sacristy
Pasqualino Veneto
Madonna of Milk, XV c.

50. Sacristy
Jacopo da Ponte called Jacopo Bassano
St John the Baptist in the Desert, 1566

51. Sacristy
Rocco Marconi
Virgin and Child with Saints Jerome and Francis, XVI c.

52. Sacristy
Lazzaro Bastiani
Virgin and Child, XV c.

53-55. Sacristy
Giuseppe Briati
Reliquaries, 1755

54. Sacristy
Our Lady Glykophilousa (of Tenderness), XVII c.

Origins

The origin of the Redentore votive church is linked to the plague that devastated Venice between 1575-77, claiming almost fifty thousand lives. The Senate decreed construction of a church dedicated to the Redeemer which was to become a permanent place of annual pilgrimage in thanks at having survived the scourge. The work was assigned to Andrea Palladio, while after much discussion the choice of location eventually fell on the site of the Santa Maria degli Angeli Chapel on the island of Giudecca. This church was served by the Capuchin friars from the nearby hermitage who, accepting to officiate free of charge at the new church, were concerned at its majesty. They asked that their vote of poverty be respected, the simplicity of their hermitage be maintained, and that the church of Christ's Passion and Resurrection not be host to noble burials; a practice that enriched the other churches of the city and often the orders that looked after them. It was precisely this request and the resulting commitment from the government that prevented tampering in the Baroque age, the main reason for the present extraordinary stylistic-decorative unity of the church.

Exterior

Seen from the front, from the riva delle Zattere opposite, the external mass is dominated and co-ordinated by the dome. Palladio brought the long reflections of Renaissance architects, starting with Leon Battista Alberti's theories and practice on the manner of adapting elements of the classical temple to a Christian church, to a conclusion in the façade. His solution in this case was completely related to the votive nature of the church. Almost a pronaos, the classical façade advances in the foreground to receive the ducal procession in a single, enlarged fornix. This procession is still repeated annually on the third Sunday of July, crossing the Giudecca Canal on a votive bridge.

A staircase as wide as the diameter of the dome – the canon for the entire building – offers a double reference: to the podium of the Vitruvian temple and, with its fifteen steps, to the temple of Jerusalem. The tympanum corresponding to the nave is supported on two Composite demi-columns and two pilasters; the lower and wider one by four Corinthian lesenes with an entablature elevated to support the tympanum above the doorway, resting on demi-columns. A final, simple hint

Nave

Side chapels

of tympanum, higher up, corresponds to and 'hides' the buttresses of the side chapels. There are two aediculae with curved gables on small Corinthian lesenes in the intercolumniation of the larger order. The seven statues date from after 1673.

Interior

The longitudinally arranged church is a co-ordination of three different spatial cells: the high, barrel vaulted nave illuminated by thermal windows and with deep side chapels; a chancel space with large apses, almost echoing a transept and separated from the nave by a large triumphal arch; and a simple rectangular choir, screened by an exedra of tall columns that emphasises the central position of the chancel. The architectural structure in this way conceptually expresses the votive and processional function of the church. Building work was completed in 1592. The font of the Redeemer's Blood at the centre of the chancel retains all its significance even from the frontal position of someone looking from the nave, providing the hub of the iconographic plan followed by the circle of chapels. Beginning on the right of the entrance, the great Christian mysteries unfold, linked to the original significance of the church. The key element is the light.

The choir

The five windows illuminating the choir create the scenographic effect of placing the figure of the Crucifix almost in backlight and suggesting an adjoining but separate illuminated room. A space of austere simplicity lies beyond the diaphragm of four columns marking the curve of the central apse, with its clear volumetry and the sober lines of its eighteenth century wooden benches.

Palma Giovane

The *Transport of Christ to the Sepulchre* is composed in overlying registers: Mary and the pious women in the foreground with Christ being taken to the tomb above. The scene is characterised by an accentuated pathos. The mother has by now felt the sword which, according to prophecy, would pierce her heart; one of the pious woman lays a knowing hand on her breast. There is a clear contrast between the sorrowful and abandoned body of the dead Christ, and the strong, vigorous, lively figure of Joseph of Arimathea. The livid flesh and the white of the shroud are in strong chromatic opposition to the head of the dark-haired youth, with brown coloured limbs and red clothing.
A source of transcendental light coming down from above shines out from the body of Christ, illuminating the characters in theatrical attitudes with flashes. Jacopo's studies in this period were predominantly into the use of light; accompanied here by a compositional structure powerfully built up from below, a warm palette and mellow pictorial matter.

Sacristy

This small, intimate room houses numerous works of art. The panel by Alvise Vivarini is set like a red gemstone in a precious reliquary frame of carved and gilt wood, decorated with winged putti on the outer band, with volutes, festoons, flowers and fruit. This is probably contemporary with the painting, dated around 1500 – during the artist's last period of activity. At this time he was already reinterpreting the themes typical of his family's tradition (of his father Antonio and uncle Bartolomeo) in a Renaissance manner, under the powerful influence of Giovanni Bellini. In this absorbed Virgin, dressed in a bright red cloak woven with threads of gold, the light models the solid, architectural volumes, softens the flesh tones and gives a velvety touch to the symbolic fruit resting on the balustrade.

The canvas with the *Virgin and Child with Saints* by Palma Giovane is in a precious seventeenth-century, wooden, gilt frame decorated with volutes and foliage. Almost twenty years separate this from the *Deposition*, providing the opportunity to see a different aspect of Palma's work, in this phase influenced by Titian, marked by an intended archaism that seems to also echo the manner of Palma Vecchio.

The *Virgin and Child* is an original bronze sculpture attributed to Jacopo Sansovino. Mary covers the Child laid next to her on a rock with her cloak. She is caught in the act of standing up, as if to more easily watch over her sleeping son. The composition and the Virgin's pose are completely unnatural, suggesting a work conceived on models from outside the Veneto, possibly in the manner of Donatello.

The Passion and its symbols: Vivarini, Bastiani, Bissolo, Marconi, Palma, Sansovino

The premonition of the Passion is a recurring theme in Venetian painting, powerfully present in the works housed in the sacristy of the Redentore. Fifteenth century artists assigned this explicitly to the symbols of the Passion, placed alongside the Virgin and the Child.

But in his *Virgin* Alvise Vivarini employs the grand innovation of Giovanni Bellini, entrusting the presentiment to the gathered structure of the forms, to the silence in which the figures seem suspended and to the suffused melancholy of their facial expressions. In iconographic tra-

45. Paolo Caliari called Veronese
Baptism of Christ
c. 1561

11. **Francesco Bassano**
Resurrection of Christ, XVI c.

dition the sleep of the Child prefigures his death, while his defenceless nudity alludes to his humanity offered in sacrifice. Anticipating the images of the Pietà, the mother takes him on her knee as if on an altar, and her hands meet in protection as if a tabernacle. The baluster touched by the external light, the table and the altar separating us from the sacred area, which at the same time connects to our space through the mediation of the two angel musicians, refer to the sacrificial and Eucharistic significance. The not unequivocal meaning of the fruit also belongs to this intermediation between the human and divine worlds: the apple taken by Adam, but it is also an allusion to Christ, the fruit of grace hanging from the cross. The thistle-finch recurs often in these subjects. It was traditionally regarded as a courageous bird, unafraid of hurting itself in order to eat the sharp thistles to which it owes its name. Spiny thistles, sufferings and thorns as the fruit of sin emerge from the parched earth for Adam and Eve. The thistle-finch, which pours its blood over them, alludes gently to the redeeming sacrifice of Christ.

50. Jacopo da Ponte called Jacopo Bassano
St John the Baptist in the Desert
1566

Lazzaro Bastiani's *Virgin and Child* shows a more limited but more direct symbology. The naked, chipped stone is also the stone of the sepulchre and the altar. The message is once more entrusted mainly to formal choices, to the sad elegy of that white trickle that frames the thoughtful face of the mother.

In the works of Francesco Bissolo, Rocco Marconi and Palma Giovane, the focal point is left to a recurring pose, to the hand with which Mary squeezes the foot of her son in anticipation of the nail that will pass through it.

Finally, in the bronze group attributed to Sansovino, the sculptor gives an intense expression to the face of this mother. Her participation in the sacrifice of her son may be glimpsed in the gesture that is perhaps to wake the Child sleeping on a rock or perhaps to enfold him as in a shroud.

Santa Maria del Rosario (Gesuati)

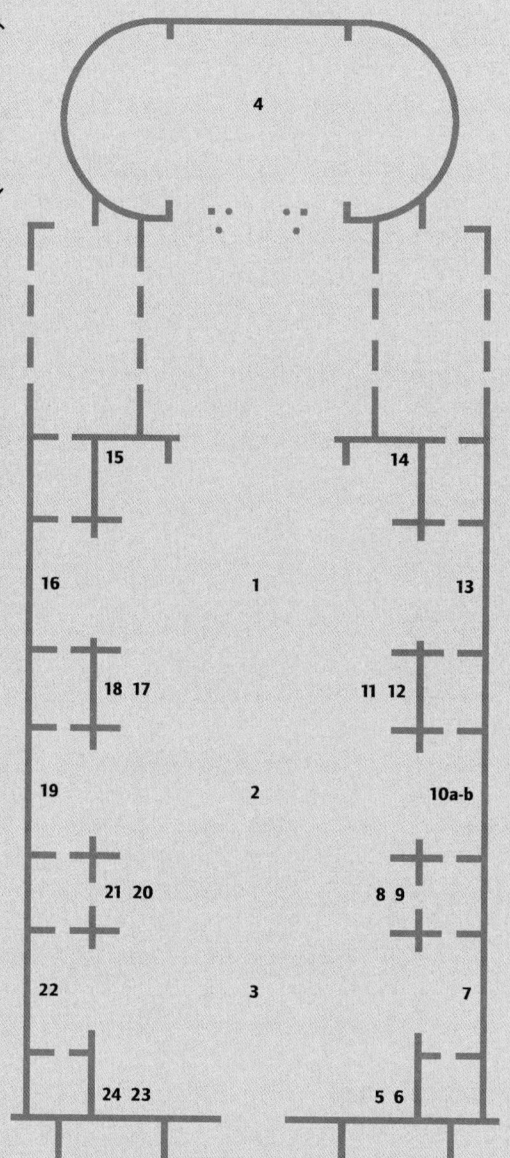

1. Giambattista Tiepolo
Apparition of the Virgin to St Dominic, 1737-39

2. Giambattista Tiepolo
Institution of the Rosary
1737-39

3. Giambattista Tiepolo
Glory of St Dominic, 1737-39

4. Choir Ceiling
Giambattista Tiepolo
David plays the Harp
1737-39

5. Gian Maria Morlaiter
Abraham, 1754

6. Gian Maria Morlaiter
Jesus and the Centurion
1754

7. Giambattista Tiepolo
The Virgin appears to Saints Rose of Lima, Catherine of Siena and Agnes of Montepulciano, 1748

8. Gian Maria Morlaiter
Aaron, 1750

9. Gian Maria Morlaiter
Christ healing the Blind
1750

10a. Gian Maria Morlaiter
Glory of Angels, 1739

10b. Giambattista Piazzetta
St Dominic, 1743

11. Gian Maria Morlaiter
St Paul the Apostle, 1747

12. Gian Maria Morlaiter
Jesus appears to the Magdalene, 1743

13. Giambattista Piazzetta
Vision of Saints Luis Bertrand, Vincent Ferrer and Hyacinth, 1738

14. Gian Maria Morlaiter
Apparition of Jesus to Thomas, 1747

15. Gian Maria Morlaiter
Baptism of Christ, 1746

16. Jacopo Tintoretto
Crucifixion, c. 1565

17. Gian Maria Morlaiter
St Peter, 1744

18. Gian Maria Morlaiter
The Samaritan at the Well
1744

19. Antonio Bosa
Madonna of the Rosary
1836

20. Gian Maria Morlaiter
Moses, 1748-50

21. Gian Maria Morlaiter
The Pool of Bethesda
1748-50

22. Sebastiano Ricci
Saints Pius V, Thomas of Aquinas and Peter Martyr
1730-33

23. Gian Maria Morlaiter
Melchisedech, 1755

24. Gian Maria Morlaiter
St Peter saved from the Waters, 1755

Origins

The establishment of the lay Gesuati Order at Zattere in the parish of Sant'Agnese is documented from 1397. Originally from Siena, the Gesuati managed to occupy various spaces thanks to several testamentary bequests, and in 1493 finally commissioned construction of their convent church. This is still extant, alongside the big eighteenth-century building designed by Massari. The small church, now known as Santa Maria della Visitazione, is a simple but accomplished example of high-Renaissance architecture. The Order was suppressed by Pope Clement IX in 1668 following a reduction in members and lack of callings, and the convent put up for sale.

It was bought by the Dominicans, who established themselves there and continued to officiate in the small annex church. Shortly after, however, the space became too small and thoughts turned to a new and larger temple. The plan by Giorgio Massari was chosen in 1724, after the death of the first designer involved, and it was with precisely this wide-ranging design that he made his debut on the Venetian artistic scene. There is no doubt at all that Massari was responsible not only for the church, but also for all the external and internal decoration: from the altars and statues through to the pews and floor. The result is a complete, consistent design that makes the chiesa dei Gesuati one of the most interesting examples of eighteenth-century Venetian art.

The new church

In designing the new church, Massari found himself having to reckon – even if only virtually – with a great adversary: Andrea Palladio. Indeed, the chiesa dei Gesuati is located right in front of three big works by the famous sixteenth-century architect: San Giorgio Maggiore, the Zitelle and especially the Redentore, almost representing their direct visual extension. Massari resolved the problem by designing a façade that is strongly inspired by the work of his famous predecessor. Big Corinthian semi-columns mark the rhythm, while the whole is crowned by a triangular tympanum; the only concession to decoration being the four big statues in niches. These are by Venetian sculptors, including Torretto, and represent the four cardinal virtues: justice, prudence, strength and temperance. Contrary to the custom of the time, Massari did not sacrifice the small church of the Visitazione when building the new church, and this can still be seen; neither did he forget to provide adequate water access, adding a new staircase to the embankment. The interior of the church has a single, rectangular nave, rounded off in the corners, with lateral altars – three on each side – and a deep, square chancel, raised by a few steps and covered with a dome, with choir behind. The brightness of the church, ensured by big thermal windows on both

Giorgio Massari
Front over the Giudecca Canal

sides, and the splendid polychrome marble floor make this a place of gracious elegance. Only a few years passed from the laying of the first stone, in 1726, to when the church could be said to have been completed, in 1735, with construction of the roof and two simple bell-towers, also of Palladian inspiration. All that remained to finish the work was the interior decoration.

The ceiling decorations

It is certain that the decorations were designed directly by Massari, with the assistance of two other great Venetian artists: Giambattista Tiepolo and Gian Maria Morlaiter, and an important contribution from the Dominican priests regarding the iconography. The result was one of great artistic and spiritual harmony.

All the pictorial decorations in the church are centred on the celebration of the Order of Dominicans. The first work completed by Giambattista was the fresco decoration of the ceiling between 1737 and 1739, with three big panels depicting the *Apparition of the Virgin to St Dominic*, the *Institution of the Rosary* and the *Glory of St Dominic*, and sixteen monochromes with the *Mysteries of the Rosary* and *Putti*. There is another monochrome above the door showing the *Vision of St Pius V*. In addition to these, he painted a further twelve monochromes in the bays at the sides of the windows, the frescoes in the dome above the main altar, and the ceiling and one wall of the choir. Later, in 1748, he also completed the altarpiece portraying three Dominican saints: Rose of Lima, Catherine of Siena and Agnes of Montepulciano. With this work Tiepolo became definitively established in Venice as one of the greatest painters of his time.

The three ceiling panels represent the most important episodes in the life of the Order's founder. The first, the *Apparition of the Virgin to St Dominic*, recounts the episode in which the Virgin, opening her cloak, allowed the saint to glimpse the glories of the Order he founded and a multitude of future disciples, including several Blessed. The Virgin appears from a cloud that opens up in the middle of a big patch of blue sky, above a high marble podium; St Dominic is at the foot of the podium, with his symbols, the lily, the greyhound and the book, on the steps at his feet.

The second panel, portraying the *Institution of the Rosary*, originates in the elevation of the Rosary festival to a universal celebration by Pope Clement XI in 1714, and recounts two fundamental episodes from the life of St Dominic: the consignment of the Rosary by the Virgin and his preaching in France. According to tradition, the Virgin appeared to St Dominic to give him the Rosary which was to be his weapon for defeat-

Main altar

7. Giambattista Tiepolo
The Virgin appears to Saints Rose of Lima, Catherine of Siena and Agnes of Montepulciano, 1748

20. Gian Maria Morlaiter
Moses, 1748-50

1-3. Giambattista Tiepolo
Ceiling, 1737-39: *Glory of St Dominic*; *Institution of the Rosary*; *Apparition of the Virgin to St Dominic*

ing the Albigensian heresy – from Albi, the Provençal town where the sect was formed. The Albigensians promoted very close adherence to the scriptures and a return of the clergy to the poverty of their origins. After this episode, Dominic dedicated himself to preaching, founding his Order and converting numerous Albigensians and speaking to all, rich and poor. Tiepolo makes use of a considerably foreshortened perspective and a broad stairway with fifteen steps – the mysteries of the Rosary – for the composition, with Dominic at the centre and the Virgin on the left. The crowd that gathers around to receive the Rosaries from the hands of the saint is arranged in various groups. On the left, the figure of a doge, that of a Dominican nun and of a simple woman holding a child represent Dominic's preaching to all social classes. On the saint's right is a crowd of Orientals and warriors. Several figures are falling at the bottom of the composition; amongst these, one has snakes in his hands and amongst his hair while another falls grasping a pouch of coins between his hands. Just above, a halberdier probes the space with a leg in a very daring posture.

The third panel shows the *Glory of St Dominic*, in which the saint is being conducted to eternal beatitude by a flight of angels, leaving his symbols on the ground. An angel dressed in red acts as a counterbalance to the dark mass of ground on the left. In these paintings, Giambattista experimented with a new use of Veronese-inspired colour: abandoning vivid, brilliant tones in favour of a very light chromatic texture, with clear, pale and, at the same time, iridescent colours.

Piazzetta and Tiepolo at the Gesuati

While Tiepolo was decorating the ceiling, Piazzetta, always his main rival, painted an altarpiece with the *Vision of Saints Luis Bertrand, Vincent Ferrer and Hyacinth* in 1738 for the third altar on the right. This is one of the most interesting works by the artist and dates from his best period, marked by the particular brightness of the colour. Luis Bertrand is portrayed at bottom left at the moment of his revelation, when he heard a voice say: 'you still live in darkness; a time will come when you will be given great splendour'. It was the moment when the saint abandoned the darkness to reach the splendour of the Lord. The saint is depicted with extraordinary realism, his face bony and hands skeletal from the efforts of a lifetime preaching and the tortures suffered under the natives of the Caribbean.

16. Jacopo Tintoretto
Crucifixion, c. 1565

13. Giambattista Piazzetta
Vision of Saints Luis Bertrand, Vincent Ferrer and Hyacinth
1738

22. Sebastiano Ricci
Saints Pius V, Thomas of Aquinas and Peter Martyr
1730-33

The snake emerging from the chalice alludes to one of these tortures: the saint was poisoned with cobra venom but was saved after days of suffering. In the centre, in white, is Vincent Ferrer, with his arms spread in the moment of ecstasy and his symbol, the small flame, burning on his forehead. On the right, St Hyacinth dressed in an ash-grey habit holds a Host in an eighteenth-century ostensory in one hand and a statue of the Virgin in the other: his weapons for preaching in the midst of the Tartars. There is a splendid play of light in the canvas, from black to white, to grey and brown.

In 1748 Giambattista painted an altarpiece for the first altar on the right depicting *The Virgin appears to Saints Rose of Lima, Catherine of Siena and Agnes of Montepulciano.* Although having the same classical layout as the Dominican altarpieces, it is clear that Giambattista was also influenced by Piazzetta's preceding composition, from which it does not deviate, possibly also due to the intervention of the Dominican priests. The theme of this canvas is the worship of the Infant Jesus, focal point of the three saints' moral life and the sublimation of maternity. The figure of St Rose of Lima, only recently canonized, dominates in the centre with the Infant in her arms, just received from St Agnes, and whom she is about to pass on to St Catherine. The Infant squeezes her thumb, in a tender, infantile gesture, while the three women are engrossed in the ecstasy of contemplation. The Virgin watches the scene seated on a fiery cloud wearing a red dress and blue cloak, which contrast with the brilliant white of Catherine and Rose's garments, and the deep black – synthesis of all colours – of Agnes' cloak.

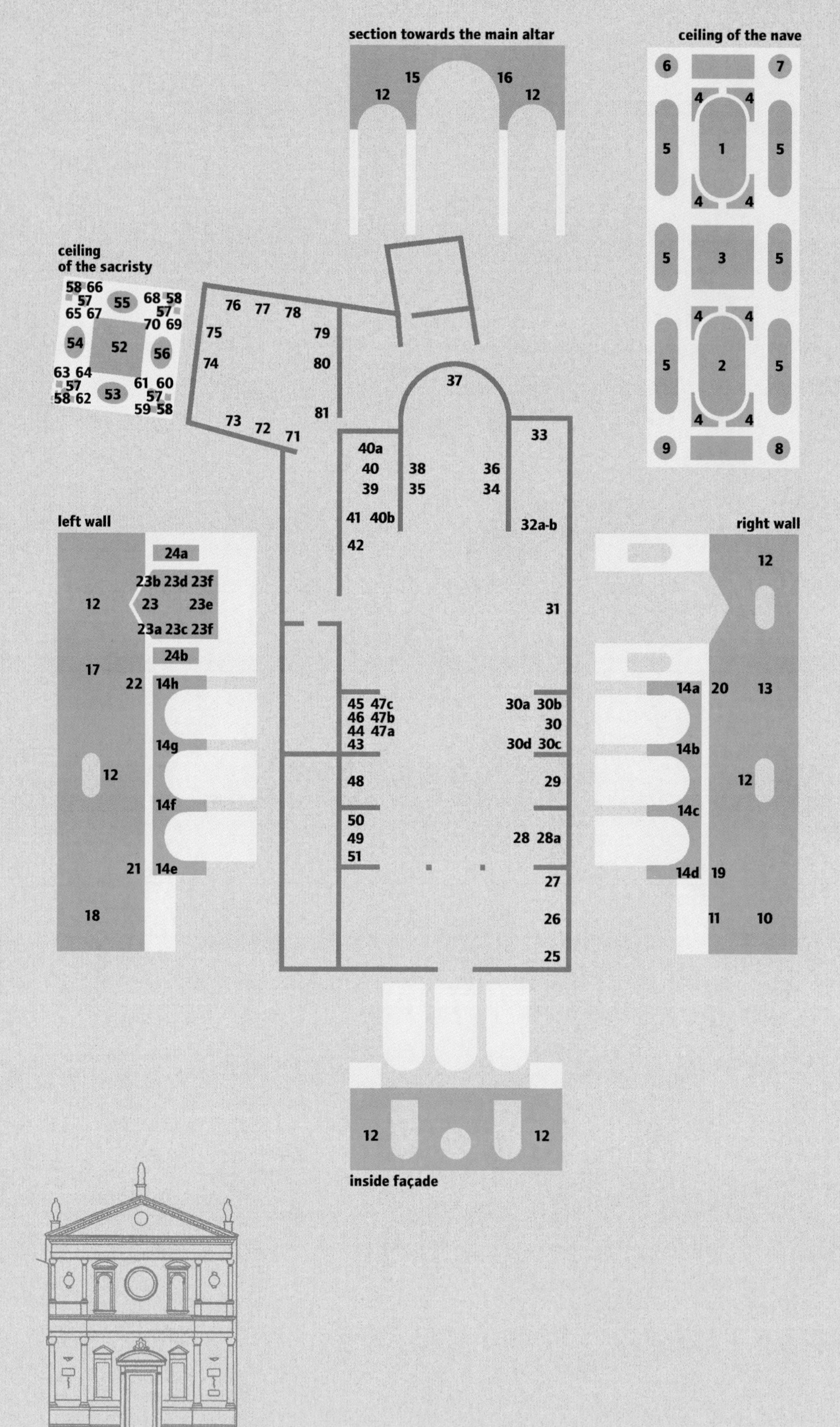

section towards the main altar
12 15 16 12
ceiling of the nave
6 7
4 4
5 1 5
4 4
5 3 5
4 4
5 2 5
4 4
9 8
ceiling
of the sacristy
58 66 57 55 68 58 57
65 67 70 69
54 52 56
63 64 57 61 60 57
58 62 53 59 58
76 77 78
75 79
74 80
81
73 72 71
37
33
40a
40 38 36
39 35 34
41 40b
32a-b
42
31
45 47c 30a 30b
46 47b 30
44 47a
43 30d 30c
48 29
50
49 28 28a
51
27
26
25
left wall
24a
23b 23d 23f
12 23 23e
23a 23c 23f
24b
17
22 14h
14g
12
14f
21 14e
18
right wall
12
14a 20 13
14b
12
14c
14d 19
11 10
12 12
inside façade

1-9. CEILING OF THE NAVE
Paolo Caliari
called Veronese, 1556
- *Triumph of Mordechai*
- *The Repudiation of Vashti*
- *Esther crowned by Ahasuerus*
- *Angels supporting the cornices*
- *Decorations with flowers and fruit*
- *Hope*
- *Justice*
- *Faith*
- *Charity*

10-14a-h-18.
WALLS OF THE NAVE
Paolo Caliari called Veronese
- *St Sebastian before Diocletian*, 1558
- *Friar leaving the Choir*, 1558
- *Solomonic culumn freize with figures of prophets and sibyls*, 1558
- *St Sebastian pierced by the Arrows*, 1558
- *St Luke*, c. 1560
- *St Matthew*, c. 1560
- *St Thomas*, c. 1560
- *Apostle with Scroll*, c. 1560
- *Apostle with Chalice*, c. 1560
- *St James*, c. 1560
- *St Andrew*, c. 1560
- *St Peter*, c. 1560
- *Announcing Angel*, c. 1558
- *Virgin Annunciata*, c. 1558
- *Three Archers*, 1558
- *Martyrdom of St Sebastian* 1558

19-22. WALLS OF THE NAVE
Gerolamo Campagna, c. 1580
statues on the balustrade
- *Cumaean Sibyl*
- *Virgin Annunciata*
- *Eritrean Sibyl*
- *Announcing Angel*

23. NAVE
Francesco Fiorentino
Organ, 1558-60

23a-b/ c-d/ e-f/ 24a-b.
NAVE
Paolo Caliari
called Veronese, 1558-60
- *Presentation at the Temple*, organ doors closed
- *Pool of Bethesda*, organ doors open
- *Nativity*
- *Figures of Virtues*
- *Isaiah*
- *David*

25. NAVE
Anonymous, *Deposition*, XV c.

26. NAVE
Paris Bordone (attr.)
Jonah and the Whale, XVI c.

27. NAVE
Tiziano Vecellio
St Nicholas, 1563

28. NAVE
Anonymous, *Christ in Glory*
altar frontal, XVI c.

28a. NAVE
Federico Bencovich
The Blessed Pietro Gambacorta, 1725-30

29. NAVE
Tommaso Lombardi da Lugano
Virgin and Child with the Infant St John, 1571

30. NAVE
Paolo Caliari called Veronese
Crucifixion, 1581

30a-d. NAVE
Pietro Baratta, XVII c.
- *Christ*
- *St Joseph*
- *St Anne*
- *The Virgin*

31. NAVE
Jacopo Tatti called Sansovino
Monument to Bishop Livio Podacattaro, 1556-57

32a-b. RIGHT APSIDAL CHAPEL
Andrea Michieli
called Vicentino, XVI c.
- *Episode from the Life of St Charles*
- *Episode from the Life of St Jerome*

33. RIGHT APSIDAL CHAPEL
Jacopo Negretti
called Palma Giovane
Virgin and Child with Saints Charles and Jerome, c. 1620

34-35. CHANCEL
Anonymous, XVI c.
- *The Evangelists Mark and Luke*
- *The Evangelists Matthew and John*

36-38. CHANCEL
Paolo Caliari called Veronese
- *Martyrdom of St Sebastian* 1565
- *Virgin in Glory with Saints Sebastian, Peter, Catherine and Francis*, c. 1562
- *Saints Mark and Marcellinus taken to be martyred*, 1565

39. LEFT APSIDAL CHAPEL
Faience work
Majolica paving, 1510

40. LEFT APSIDAL CHAPEL
Anonymous, *Annunciation*
altar frontal, XVII c.

40a-40b.
LEFT APSIDAL CHAPEL
Matteo Ingoli, XVI c.
Annunciation
Flight into Egypt

41. LEFT APSIDAL CHAPEL
Anonymous
Birth of the Virgin, XVI-XVII c.

42. NAVE
Matteo Cornero
Bust of Paolo Veronese, 1588

43-45. GRIMANI CHAPEL
Alessandro Vittoria
- *Bust of Marcantonio Grimani*, XVI c.
- *St Mark*, c. 1565
- *St Anthony*, c. 1565

46. GRIMANI CHAPEL
Paolo Caliari called Veronese
Virgin and Child, St Catherine and Brother Spaventi, XVI c.

47a-c. GRIMANI CHAPEL
Andrea Meldolla
called Schiavone
- *Christ praying in the Olive Grove*
- *Juda's Betrayal*
- *Deposition in the Sepulchre* c. 1540

48. NAVE
Benedetto Caliari
Baptism of Christ, XVI c.

49-51. NAVE
Andrea Meldolla
called Schiavone
- *Christ in Emmaus*, c. 1545
- *Figures of Virtues*, c. 1540
- *Figures of Virtues*, c. 1540

52-70. CEILING OF THE SACRISTY
Paolo Caliari
called Veronese, 1555
- *Coronation of the Virgin*
- *St John*
- *St Luke*
- *St Mark*
- *St Matthew*
- *Four tondi with cherubs*
- *The four cardinal Virtues*
- *Esther and Ahasuerus*
- *Moses receiving the Ten Commandments*
- *Expulsion from the Garden of Eden*
- *Judith and Holofernes*
- *Abraham and Melchisedech*
- *Creation of Eve*
- *Moses praying with the Amalekites*
- *Cain and Abel*
- *The Original Sin*
- *Judgement of Solomon*
- *David and Goliath*
- *Discovery of the Original Sin*

71-72. SACRISTY
Marten de Vos, XVI c.
- *Sacrifice of Isaac*
- *Baptism of Christ*

73. SACRISTY
Circle of Bonifacio de' Pitati
Christ praying in the Olive Grove, XVI c.

74. SACRISTY
Antonio Palma
Resurrection, XVI c.

75. SACRISTY
Anonymous, style of Tintoretto
Chastising the Serpents, XVI c.

76. SACRISTY
Anonymous
St Sebastian, XVI c.

77. SACRISTY
Domenico Brusasorci
Crucifixion, XVI c.

78. SACRISTY
Anonymous
St Paul the Hermit, XVI c.

79-81. SACRISTY
Workshop of Bonifacio de' Pitati, XVI c.
- *Jacob's Dream*
- *The Parting of the Red Sea*
- *Nativity*

Origins

The anchorite monks of San Gerolamo, the Gerolamini, founded a small monastery and hospice for the poor in 1396 on the island of Angelo Raffaele, defined by rio di San Basilio and rio di Santa Margherita. An oratory dedicated to Santa Maria Assunta also rose next to it, to be replaced by a larger church in the second half of the fifteenth century. This too was dedicated to Mary, but also to St Sebastian, protector against the plague, as a thanksgiving from the local inhabitants for deliverance from the epidemic of 1464. Jacopo de' Barbari's map from around the year 1500, an 'aerial' view of Venice, shows the façade of the building facing onto a narrow *campo*, and a side wall turned towards the rio, confirming the prevailing tendency up to the fifteenth century of orienting buildings towards the squares.

The new church

In about 1506, Antonio Abbondi, called Scarpagnino, designed a larger building which, rotated 90 degrees, significantly changed the urban layout. The main façade looked onto the rio, giving access via a bridge to the long calle dell'Avogaria, and therefore favouring the link with the city, abandoning the more local, isolated situation of the first church. The work was completed in 1548.

The church and large convent next door were suppressed in 1810 by the Napoleonic government. The church was later reopened as a branch of San Trovaso and then of Angelo Raffaele, while the convent was partly demolished and in 1856 rebuilt as a mother house for the nuns of San Giuseppe. The latter then moved into the building next door and, in 1971, the building was taken over by the University of Venice.

Interior

Renaissance style dominates both interior and exterior in this example of a *Saalkirche*: a single hall church. The large, bright, square chancel ends in a semicircular apse, is topped with a dome and flanked by two deep, narrow chapels. The first section of the nave, about two thirds of its length, is bounded by three chapels on each side, roofed by the lateral wings of the barco dei frati, a hanging monks' choir, which, describing a U shape, creates an entrance vestibule separated from the rest of the church by three arches.

37. Paolo Caliari called Veronese
The Virgin in Glory with Saints Sebastian, Peter, Catherine and Francis, c. 1562

Exterior

The internal dimensions are repeated on the façade with its facing of Istrian stone. The sloping roofed frontage is divided into three horizontal and three vertical sections with two superimposed orders supporting the different entablatures. The lower of these corresponds to the internal height of the choir, while the third horizontal section is made up of a tympanum and three acroterial statues: St Jerome, St Sebastian and St Catherine of Alexandria. The depth of the internal chapels determines the intercolumniation of the small paired columns which, on high pedestals, define a central zone about three times the width of the side chapels. The entrance door with curved gable opens in the lower part of this middle zone, along with two simple windows with triangular gables. On the upper level a circular oeil-de-boeuf is flanked by two arched windows in rectangular frames crowned with curved gables.

Paolo Caliari called Veronese

The internal decoration is marked by an extraordinary unity, determined by the cycle of works throughout the church painted by Paolo Veronese between 1555 and 1570. Overall, this is undoubtedly the largest and most important work of his life, even though set alongside such works as the decoration of the villa Barbaro in Maser, the Santi Giovanni e Paolo church and the refectory of the convent of San Giorgio Maggiore.
He painted the canvases for the lacunar ceiling of the sacristy with scenes from the Old Testament during 1555, and then that of the church through till 1556, drawing inspiration from the Book of Esther. Between 1558 and 1559 he frescoed the upper part of the nave with *Fathers of the Church*, *Prophets*, *Sibyls* and Biblical characters, the choir with *Stories of St Sebastian*, and the organ doors and parapet. Finally, between 1565 and 1570, he completed the big altarpiece and two large canvases in the chancel. There are other works of his on various altars, while some have been lost, such as the fresco of the *Assumption* in the chancel dome, or taken elsewhere. Veronese is buried under the gravestone beneath his bust by the organ.

The iconographic cycle

The ambitious project for the church's global decoration arose out of the artist's friendship with the prior Bernardo Torlioni, who had followed him from Verona. The prior was probably responsible for the thematic conception of the work, intended as an allegory of the triumph of Faith over heresy and, in the *Resurrection of Christ*, as a vision of the pos-

17. Paolo Caliari called Veronese
Three Archers, 1558

sibility of continuous victory over sin and its consequences, the plague and death. The iconographic plan brought together the inspirational motifs of the dual worship of the Virgin and St Sebastian. The Marian cycle develops according to a line of reflection based mainly on St Jerome, meaning that each episode from the Old Testament must be read in the light of a corresponding episode from the New, providing its complementary interpretation and vice versa. This is why the role of Mary in the story of salvation, victorious over death, was illustrated with the image of Esther, the Jewish queen who had saved her people from destruction.

In the *Triumph of Mordechai*, the tumultuous group of figures in the foreground, who seem to be almost falling into the church, contrasts with the dramatically foreshortened balcony in the background. This is being looked at by a group of curious people, like spectators at a theatrical presentation, and is supported by a heavy Solomonic column. Alongside, a large section of bright, empty sky expands the space beyond the confines of the visible.

In *The Repudiation of Vashti* the people appear on the slanting line of the steep staircase, while a trace of architectural elements, almost a transparent curtain in the background, coordinates the scene with the space opened up in clear sky on the side opposite that of the other oval.

In the central canvas, portraying *Esther crowned by Ahasuerus*, the space in the background is strictly symmetrical, between the open sky with its light clouds and the architectural structure on the right. The group of figures is again arranged on the diagonal, at the centre of which is Esther, richly adorned like a sixteenth century lady.

In the *Coronation of the Virgin*, the suffused, golden light from which the dove of the Holy Spirit seems to shine, invades the space between two curtains of clouds seemingly held aloft by the putti. The Virgin is kneeling on the lower clouds, while the figures of the Holy Father and of Christ stoop over her, foreshortened in the perspective of a steep bottom up view that accentuates their monumental bearing. The link between the Earthly and the Spiritual seems to be emphasised, even beyond normal iconographic standards, by the light, bright colours and the repetition of red and blue in the clothes of the Virgin and of the Son, in contrast with the harmonious greenish blue of the Holy Father.

The figures of the prophets and the sibyls record the announcement of salvation, a theme developed in the Christological cycle that intersects with the other two; in much the same way, some pagan scenes are arranged alongside the Christian symbols, in homage to Renaissance

11. Paolo Caliari called Veronese
Friar leaving the Choir, 1558

23a-b. Paolo Caliari called Veronese
Presentation at the Temple
1558-60, organ doors closed

3. Paolo Caliari called Veronese
Esther crowned by Ahasuerus, 1556

59. Paolo Caliari called Veronese
Esther and Ahasuerus, 1555

1. Paolo Caliari called Veronese
Triumph of Mordechai, 1556

culture. St Sebastian, pierced by arrows and then healed, is recognised as protector against the plague which, right from Classical and Biblical antiquity was symbolised by the unexpected arrow, shot by angry gods to punish the sins of men. He was also represented as an example of the courage of the martyr, ready to proclaim his faith and to die for it. The predominant focus of the scenography can be seen in the *Martyrdom of St Sebastian*, also presented at its climatic point. Underscored by the sudden raising of clubs on the emperor's orders, and in the contorted body of the Saint trying to protect himself from the blows, it is the theatrical nature of the story that prevails at the sake of its religious essence. This is often diluted by the artist into a very lay view of events, portrayed as contemporary occurrences. The chromatic range centres on light, transparent tones that a clear, unnatural light makes intellectual, dropping them into a suspended atmosphere, beyond the world of men. In this way, the lay humanity of Veronese's figures is removed from that of the common man, of the faithful, entering a spiritual dimension that has nothing in common with the human perspective of the observer. This standpoint is quite contrary to that of Tintoretto, who narrates the holy stories with a popular slant bringing together saint and spectator in a common world to which both belong.

Printed by
Grafiche Nardin, Ca' Savio Cavallino Treporti (Venice)
for Marsilio Editori® s.p.a. in Venezia

EDITION	YEAR
10 9 8 7 6 5 4 3 2 1	2002 2003 2004 2005 2006